The Institute of Biology's
Studies in Biology no. 39

How Trees Grow

STEPHEN L. SOLHEIM

by Philip R. Morey Ph.D.
Associate Professor of Biology
Texas Tech University

D1409682

Edward Arnold

© Philip R. Morey 1973

First published 1973
by Edward Arnold (Publishers) Limited,
25 Hill Street,
London, W1X 8LL

Boards edition ISBN: 0 7131 2385 0
Paper edition ISBN: 0 7131 2386 9

All Rights Reserved. No part of this publication may be
reproduced, stored in a retrieval system, or transmitted,
in any form or by any means, electronic, mechanical,
photocopying, recording or otherwise, without the prior
permission of Edward Arnold (Publishers) Limited.

Printed in Great Britain by
William Clowes & Sons, Limited
London, Beccles and Colchester

General Preface to the Series

It is no longer possible for one textbook to cover the whole field of biology and to remain sufficiently up to date. At the same time students at school, and indeed those in their first year at universities, must be contemporary in their biological outlook and know where the most important developments are taking place.

The Biological Education Committee, set up jointly by the Royal Society and the Institute of Biology, is sponsoring, therefore, the production of a series of booklets dealing with limited biological topics in which recent progress has been most rapid and important.

A feature of the series is that the booklets indicate as clearly as possible the methods that have been employed in elucidating the problems with which they deal. Wherever appropriate there are suggestions for practical work for the student. To ensure that each booklet is kept up to date, comments and questions about the contents may be sent to the author or the Institute.

1973

INSTITUTE OF BIOLOGY
41 Queen's Gate
London, S.W.7

Preface

The literature on tree growth is so diverse that the non-specialist is seldom able to obtain a broad appreciation of the subject. This book explains the basic developmental processes underlying tree growth including extension and radial growth of the stem and root, and the formation of the bark. The structure of wood and the developmental sequence involved in the differentiation of the woody cell wall is also described. Finally there is a consideration of the origin of tree growth as seen in the fossil record.

The approach of this book is intended to introduce the student, workers from other disciplines and the interested layman, to contemporary research on the growth of woody plants. It is hoped that the questions raised in this short review will cause the reader to examine the references suggested for further reading.

Lubbock, Texas, 1973

P.R.M.

Contents

1.1 Morphology of height growth

Trees of the temperate latitudes exhibit varied forms of shoot growth, but in general four basic patterns are recognized (ZIMMERMANN and BROWN, 1971). In the first type, height growth occurs in a *single flush* as in maple, ash, horse-chestnut, fir and in some pines (e.g. *Pinus lambertiana*). The overwintering terminal bud contains all organ primordia, preformed in an embryonic state. In spring, the bud opens and the shoot undergoes extension growth and maturation. Normally height growth of this type is restricted to a single period early in the growing season. By contrast in other pines, such as *Pinus taeda*, growth is *recurrent* with two or more distinct flushes of extension growth separated by periods of inactivity. A third pattern of shoot growth, termed *continuous*, occurs in trees (e.g. *Ginkgo*) where maturation of the preformed telescoped shoot may be followed immediately by further extension growth including both the initiation and development of new foliage leaves. Lastly, in lilac, locust, elm, etc., the upper portion of the shoot tip, after bud break and a period of extension growth, is regularly *aborted*. An upper axillary bud then replaces the aborted leader, and the shoot axis develops in a typical y-shaped or *sympodial* growth pattern.

We will consider here in detail the developmental sequence occurring in the buds of black hickory (Central USA), white fir and sugar pine (fir and pine species, Western USA), all of which normally exhibit only a single annual flush of growth in height.

The shoot system of black hickory (*Carya buckleyi* var. *arkansana*) is monopodial in that the conspicuous main stem bears short lateral branches arising from axillary buds, at some distance below the shoot tip. The dominant axis is known as the *long shoot* whereas the laterals are the *short shoots*. Terminal buds of long shoots contain, from the outside in, 9–11 bud scales, 5–11 foliage leaf primordia, and immediately adjacent to the apical meristem, 2 additional, small bud scale primordia (FOSTER, 1931). Bud scales or *cataphylls* (Niederblatt – lower leaf; ROMBERGER, 1963) are modified leaves, the main function of which is to prevent desiccation of the overwintering bud when soil moisture is unavailable to the root system due to freezing. The regular occurrence of zones of closely placed bud scale scars along the stem marks the extent of the annual increment of height growth (Fig. 1–1). The considerable distance between leaf scars on long shoots indicates the extensive elongation of internodes between successively formed foliage leaves.

The overwintering terminal bud of short shoots of black hickory contains, with regularity, 9 outer cataphylls, 4 foliage primordia and 2 pri-

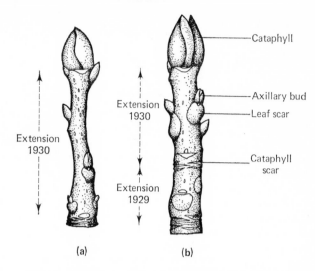

Fig. 1–1 Morphology of long and short shoots of black hickory. (a) Long shoot; × 1.05 actual size. (b) Short shoot showing two years of extension growth. The internodes are shorter here than in long shoots, × 1.8 actual size. (After FOSTER, 1931, Figs. 1 and 2, Plate 63.)

mordial cataphylls, an organization readily facilitating experimental investigation (FOSTER, 1932).

The terminal buds of short shoots commence swelling on March 22, and from that date until April 22, the outer cataphylls gradually bend backward and thus expose the young, still unextended, foliage leaves. Internode elongation and maturation of leaves on the new shoot become well advanced by mid-April and at the end of the month the cataphylls have abscised. During the period when the shoot is undergoing visible growth activities, organogenetic events occur in rapid succession in the apical meristem. In late March at the time of bud swelling, the two primordia overwintering next to the apical meristem begin to undergo maturation into cataphylls which in the next terminal bud will occupy the outermost position. Seven additional cataphylls are initiated by mid-April. Subsequently four foliage primordia followed by two small cataphyll primordia are developed. By mid-May the new terminal bud, now well exposed by unfolding and extension of the current-year-shoot, contains the expected 9 outer cataphylls, 4 foliage primordia and 2 rudimentary, inner cataphylls. Organogenetic activities of the apical meristem now cease until next spring. Terminal bud formation in black hickory is thus restricted to the period from mid-March to mid-May, only a short portion of the growing season available in Oklahoma.

In white fir (*Abies concolor*) the overwintering terminal bud consists of 20–30 cataphylls surrounding a telescoped shoot with 50–60 needle pri-

mordia (Fig. 1–2, PARKE, 1959). Bud break begins in April with the extension of foliar internodes of the telescoped shoot. As a result the cataphylls
which tightly cover the rapidly extending terminal bud are detached from
their nodes and are eventually sloughed away. Only after the new shoot is
several centimetres long does the apical meristem begin its organogenetic
activities with the initiation of cataphyll primordia. This continues until
mid-June after which needle primordia are formed. The transition from the
production of cataphyll to needle primordia is correlated with both an
enlargement of the apical meristem itself and a decline in the extension

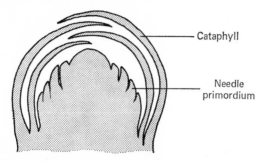

Cataphyll

Needle
primordium

Fig. 1–2 Sketch of a longitudinal section of a terminal bud of white fir showing needle primordia and cataphylls.

growth of the current-year-shoot. By September the new terminal bud
contains a telescoped shoot with 50–60 needle primordia enclosed by a
sheath of 20–30 cataphylls. In contrast to black hickory, the organogenetic
phase of development in white fir occurs for a relatively long time (most of
the growing season) and is not closely correlated with the extension activities of the current-year-shoot.

The winter bud of sugar pine (*Pinus lambertiana*) like that of white fir
contains a telescoped preformed shoot. However there are some important
constructional differences. Needle leaves are not borne directly on the main
shoot axis. Rather the organogenetic activities of the apical meristem are
continuously directed toward the formation of cataphylls which are arranged
in a precise manner from the lower to the upper portion of the unextended
bud (SACHER, 1954). The winter bud is enclosed by a number of spirally
arranged *sterile cataphylls* (without axillary bud), the outermost of which
are known as *terminal bud scales* (Fig. 1–3). The next series of cataphylls
contain in their axils short shoots on which, in turn, are formed the needle
primordia. The lateral branch system of the unextended terminal bud
originates from axillary buds of cataphylls located at still a higher position on the axis. Finally, adjacent to the apical meristem itself, a number of
sterile cataphyll primordia are found which in the next winter bud will
become terminal bud scales.

The growth of the terminal bud of sugar pine begins in early April with
the extension of the internodes of the main axis and the elongation and

rapid maturation of the needle primordia of the short shoots. Later, in the same month, the apical meristem begins to initiate new sterile cataphylls. These, together with the terminal bud scale primordia of the winter bud, mature during the growing season, and become the outer protective scales of the next overwintering terminal bud. The formation of sterile cataphylls is followed by the initiation of a series of cataphylls each of which subtends a short shoot, and then by those subtending lateral buds. Finally, as growth activity of the apical meristem decreases in the late summer, small sterile

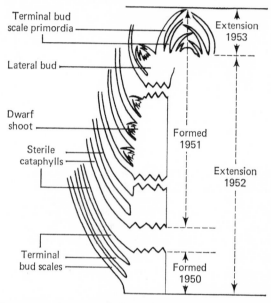

Fig. 1-3 Structure of unextended terminal bud of *Pinus*. The outermost sterile (without axillary structures) cataphylls are termed the terminal bud scales. Cataphylls progressively closer to the shoot tip bear short shoots and lateral buds respectively. Terminal bud scale primordia occur adjacent to the apical meristem. Note that terminal bud scales are initiated two years before they expand. (After SACHER, 1954, Fig. 2, p. 750.)

cataphyll primordia develop. One year later these will become the terminal bud scales of the next winter bud.

Little is known about mechanisms controlling internode elongation, and the successive seasonal production of sterile cataphylls, cataphylls subtending short shoots and lateral buds, and finally those again without axillary buds. Our knowledge is largely descriptive, but in the near future advances in our understanding are likely to occur. For further discussion and thoughtful speculation the reader is referred to the extensive treatments by ROMBERGER (1963) and ZIMMERMANN and BROWN (1971).

In some trees (as *Ginkgo, Populus*) of the temperate latitudes there is a delay in the formation of the terminal buds and shoot growth continues until late in the season. In the long shoots of *Ginkgo biloba*, the leaves expanded from the terminal bud, termed *early leaves*, differ considerably in morphology from those developed later, which are known as *late leaves* (CRITCHFIELD, 1970). This phenomenon is referred to as *heterophylly*. Early leaves in *Ginkgo* are typically unlobed or bilobed in contrast to the multilobed morphology or later foliage (Fig. 1–4). It is of interest that seedling leaves in this species resemble rather closely the morphology of late leaves on the long shoots of mature trees.

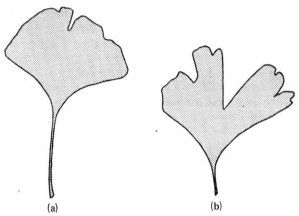

(a)　　　　　　　　　　　(b)

Fig. 1–4　Early (a) and late (b) leaves of *Ginkgo biloba*. The blade of the late leaf is highly dissected.

In both long and short shoots of *Ginkgo* all preformed leaf primordia present in winter bud develop into early leaves. Long shoots become distinguishable from short shoots, only after bud opening, when new leaf primordia are initiated and the associated internodes undergo elongation. Extension growth of the long shoot continues well into the summer before a new terminal, overwintering bud is formed. Leaves which are initiated by the apical meristem and mature during the same growing season are multilobed, late leaves. CRITCHFIELD (1970) points out that heterophylly in woody species is best understood in terms of the sequence of leaf ontogeny. The late leaves of *Ginkgo*, as well as seedling leaves, are characterized by an uninterrupted developmental sequence from initiation to maturation. On the other hand, the development of early leaves is discontinuous with a period of overwintering inactivity inserted into ontogeny between initiation and maturation.

Heterophylly may occur also in trees which are normally characterized by a single growth flush. Under exceptional growing conditions, e.g., heavy rain, a second phase of extension growth may be induced. This second flush is called a *lammas* shoot, because of its frequent coincidence with Lammas day (August 1). Leaves of the lammas shoot and the leaves formed during the normal growth flush differ in shape. Heterophylly here is likely caused by a differing ontogeny of leaf development.

1.2   Height growth in tropical trees

In spite of continuously favourable growing conditions in some regions of the tropics, most trees display an interrupted pattern of shoot growth. Thus, the cacao tree (*Theobroma cacao*) grows rhythmically, with periods of shoot extension, including all organogenetic activities, alternating with phases of inactivity (GREATHOUSE, LAETSCH and PHINNEY, 1971). Rhythmic shoot growth in cacao persists even in a controlled environmental room with a 12 hour photoperiod and a constant temperature regime, suggesting endogenous control. However, the collective shoot system of the tree shows asynchronous growth in that some branches are flushing while the others are inactive. Thus although shoot growth is rhythmic, endogenous control appears to reside in the individual branch so that, unlike trees of the temperate latitudes, shoot growth is asynchronous throughout the tree as a whole.

BORCHERT (1969) describes an interesting rhythmic pattern of shoot growth in *Oreopanax*, a tropical evergreen tree of the mountains of Colombia, in which cataphylls form as part of the normal growth sequence. During the active phase of shoot elongation large foliage leaves develop and the shoot undergoes considerable extension. Leaves formed later are progressively smaller and their subjacent internodes show less and less elongation. Finally, as the rest phase commences the shoot tip is surrounded by a rosette of leaves, the smallest bearing greatly expanded petiolar bases. Cataphylls occur at this stage only as very *small primordia* adjacent to the apical meristem. *Oreopanax* is atypical in that the shoot tip enters the resting stage while the cataphylls are immature. When growth resumes a terminal bud covered by maturing cataphylls rises from the rosette. The cataphylls and their associated internodes undergo some extension thereby elevating the developing terminal bud above the leaf rosette. Usually 6 weeks pass between the emergence of the terminal bud and its opening. During this time, when organogenetic activities are rapidly taking place, the shoot tip remains covered by the protective cataphylls. After the terminal bud opens, the new foliage shoot expands and the cataphylls are abscised. Obviously the resting shoot tip of *Oreopanax* differs from temperate-zone woody plants in that it contains no preformed embryonic foliage leaves. As a result, a rather long developmental period is necessary after rest during which the new embryonic foliage shoot is formed.

Like trees of temperate latitudes, the shoot of *Oreopanax* grows rhythmically and forms cataphylls. However, the period of rest commences before the terminal bud develops. Borchert speculates that resting buds may have arisen in areas marginal to the tropics, and that migration to the relatively constant growing conditions of the equatorial zone may have caused the complex processes involved in the formation of the typical terminal resting bud to become out of phase.

1.3 The role of auxin

It has been known for many years that auxin is involved in the extension growth of the shoot. Thus, e.g. in *Ginkgo*, diffusible auxin is obtainable from growing shoots, especially from elongating internodes, whereas, in overwintering buds, none is present.

The shoot system of *Ginkgo biloba* is composed of short shoots (about 10 mm long) and long shoots (2 to 75 cm long) (CRITCHFIELD, 1970). The early pattern of development of putative long and short shoots is markedly similar. During bud swell in early April (Massachusetts, USA) little difference is noted in size or appearance. In May when the cataphylls separate and reflex, the early leaves expand rapidly and this is accompanied by little or no internode elongation. Now the developmental pathway becomes evident as growth of the short shoot ceases with the formation of 8–14 cataphylls. By contrast, the internodes of long shoots begin to extend rapidly. Simultaneously, new foliage of the late-leaf-type is initiated by the active apical meristem. Rapid extension growth continues into June with the development of new leaves and internodes.

Diffusible auxin can be obtained from putative long and short shoot tips as soon as bud swelling becomes evident (Fig. 1–5). The level of auxin increases and reaches a peak in late April, which coincides with the differentiation of xylem in the veins of embryonic leaves still enclosed within the bud (CRITCHFIELD, 1970). Subsequently, as the bud opens, the level of diffusible auxin falls, and in short shoots, now identified by the absence of internode elongation, the decline in auxin level continues. In long shoots however, a transient dip in auxin level is followed by a very rapid increase to a new higher level, which is correlated with internode extension and new leaf production. During the rapid extension of the long shoot in June the region of maximal auxin production shifts from the shoot tip to the elongating internodes themselves, especially those in the lower portion of the elongating shoot. Auxin, thus appears to be the underlying factor mediating extension growth in long shoots of *Ginkgo*. Further experiments (Fig. 1–6) show that auxin is produced in the leaves of the long shoot.

Regulatory systems involved in the control of height growth in woody plants are ultimately involved in the control of cell division and cell elongation in the rib and peripheral meristems of the developing internode. In this regard, Brown (see references in ZIMMERMANN and BROWN, 1971) cites the interesting case of the 'grass stage' in longleaf pine (*Pinus palustris*) wherein the role of auxin in controlling internode extension is more precisely defined. In longleaf pine the leader may grow each year as a short shoot for periods of up to 15 years during which time internode elongation is rigidly inhibited. Brown observed that although auxin can be extracted

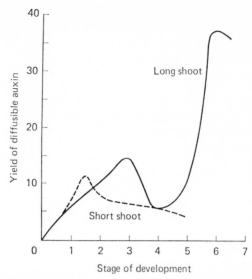

Fig. 1–5 Yield of diffusible auxin from lateral buds developing either as long or short shoots. See text for explanation. Stages of development: (1) dormant bud, (2) bud swelling, (3,4) cataphylls opening and reflexing respectively, (5) leaves expanding, (6) (long shoots only) internodes elongating and (7) long shoot extends up to 2.5 cm. (After GUNCKEL and THIMANN, 1949, Fig. 1, 2, pp. 146, 147.)

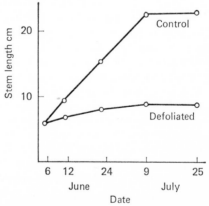

Fig. 1–6 Defoliation of developing long shoots greatly decreases extension growth. (After CRITCHFIELD, 1970, *Botanical Gazette*, Fig. 5, p. 156. Copyright © 1970 by the University of Chicago. All rights reserved.) This together with the strong reduction in yield of diffusible auxin known to result from defoliation (GUNCKEL and THIMANN, 1949) suggests that extension growth is mediated by auxin and further that auxin or an auxin precursor is produced in leaves of the long shoot.

from the short shoot leader, none can be collected by diffusion techniques. In other words, polar auxin transport appears to be absent in the grass stage; auxin cannot be diffused out of the short shoot into an agar block. Application of indole-3-acetic acid (IAA) to the shoot apex causes necrosis of the meristematic tissue, and this is most likely due to the inability of the short shoot to transport the hormone which then accumulates in toxic amounts. Clearly the short shoot during the grass stage is apolar. Diffusible auxin eventually becomes demonstrable in the leader of long-leaf pine just prior to the transition from the short to the long shoot habit. The short shoot habit thus appears correlated with the absence of polar auxin transport. The mechanism by which auxin stimulates elongation when transported in a polar manner through embryonic internodal tissue is a subject of current physiological interest but beyond the scope of this book (see WAREING and PHILLIPS, 1970).

1.4 Dormancy

Shoot growth in most woody plants is characterized by periods of in-activity or *dormancy*. In trees of the temperate latitudes dormancy can be discussed in terms of three sequential phases: *correlative inhibition*, *rest*, and *quiescence* (ROMBERGER, 1963; WAREING and PHILLIPS, 1970).

The unextended terminal bud in the summer is not truly dormant, but rather its growth is *inhibited* by the activities of other organs, as for example mature leaves. Thus the terminal bud may undergo rapid extension as a result of defoliation of the shoot by severe insect attack. The development of lammas shoots after heavy rain or fertilization is still another case of the potential growth of apparently inactive terminal buds. In the autumn the terminal bud enters *rest*, and then, in spite of experimental treatments like defoliation, extension growth does not occur. Rest is caused by conditions existing within the bud itself, and in most woody plants shoot growth will begin again only after a period of winter chilling. After rest is broken shoot growth usually remains inhibited by unfavourable environmental conditions. This period of externally imposed dormancy is known as *quiescence*. The German custom of collecting cherry twigs on St. Barbara's Day (Dec. 4) so that they will flower on Christmas Day provides a clear example of the difference between rest and quiescence (ROMBERGER, 1963). Twigs taken indoors in early December will flower, whereas those brought in earlier, in November, do not. The former were quiescent and ready to respond to favourable growing conditions. In the November collection however, rest had not yet been broken by chilling.

Shoot growth in a number of woody species is sensitive to photoperiod, with long days promoting and short days inhibiting growth (WAREING, 1969; ROMBERGER, 1963). For example, in *Robinia* seedlings exposed to short days, growth stops and later the shoot tip is abscised. If the shoot tip is given long days while the leaves are exposed to short days, extension growth still ceases. The shoot, however, shows continuous growth if the experimental conditions are reversed, suggesting that the photoperiodic response is perceived by the mature leaves. Wareing and co-workers have shown that cessation of shoot growth under short days is correlated with the production of inhibitors in the mature leaves. That this is a causal relationship is supported by experiments wherein a transition from long to short days brings about a marked increase in the inhibitor level in the shoot tip just before a terminal bud is formed (WAREING, 1969). For example, in black currant (*Ribes nigrum*) seedlings maintained under long days and then transferred to short days, the concentration of inhibitors in the shoot tip rapidly increases (WAREING and PHILLIPS, 1970). Also, the content of gibberellin declines suggesting that the onset of dormancy is governed by an increasing inhibitor/gibberellin ratio. Now, if the inhibitor and gibberellin contents are followed through a period of winter chilling, until bud break, it is found that the gibberellin concentration gradually increases whereas the inhibitor content declines. Emergence of the winter bud from rest thus is associated with a low inhibitor/gibberellin ratio.

A natural inhibitor produced in leaves in short days has been identified as the sesquiterpenoid *abscisic acid* (ABA). Application of ABA to leaves of seedlings of black currant causes a cessation of shoot growth and the formation of a terminal bud with cataphylls (WAREING and PHILLIPS, 1970). If treatment with ABA continues for several weeks the terminal bud enters rest and does not resume growth when the treatment is terminated. Recent studies indicate that ABA is involved in the onset of dormancy in many angiosperms and gymnosperms.

ABA is undoubtedly one of the controlling agents of dormancy in many trees, especially those which are sensitive to changes in photoperiod. On the other hand in other trees rhythmic shoot growth is regulated by entirely different mechanisms. For example, in *Oreopanax* (§ 1.2), Borchert (1969) questions the role of ABA in rhythmic growth since extractable inhibitors are absent throughout the entire shoot growth cycle.

Wood

2.1 Structure of wood

Wood has occupied a central position in human affairs ever since Neanderthal man employed it for fire and probably for implements and weapons. Today wood is utilized extensively in construction, papermaking and still, where easily accessible, as a fuel. Wood is formed in the stems, roots and branches of gymnosperms and arborescent angiosperms. The wood of coniferous gymnosperms (softwoods) is valued especially in papermaking and construction. On the other hand the wood of dicotyledonous angiosperms (hardwoods) is utilized in fine furniture and panelling. The terms softwood and hardwood, unfortunately well established, are not to be taken strictly as a measure of physical hardness for some hardwoods, e.g. balsa, are in fact much softer than most softwoods.

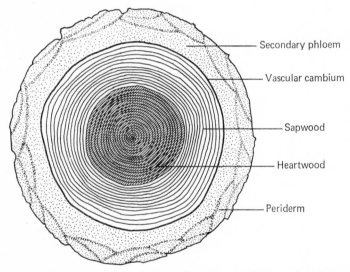

Fig. 2–1 Diagram of a transverse section of a woody stem showing major components of the wood and bark.

The secondary plant body, of which wood is the major component, is derived from activities of two lateral meristems, the vascular cambium and the phellogen or cork cambium. Examination of a section from a tree trunk with a ×10 lens provides a general orientation (Fig. 2–1). Wood, which constitutes by far the greater bulk of the section, is separated from the bark by the vascular cambium. Fusiform and ray initials (GEMMELL, 1969) of the vascular cambium give rise to the elements of the wood and the inner bark by a process of tangential division and enlargement and differentiation of the derivative cells. Bark is a non-specific term referring to all tissues outside the vascular cambium including both the secondary phloem and the periderm or, where more than one periderm occurs, the rhytidome. Only a thin layer of phloem, that part most recently differentiated from derivatives of the vascular cambium, is functional in the conduction of organic assimilates. The other major component of the bark, the periderm, is derived from a cork cambium and has a protective function (Chapter 5). The wood of some trees can be demarcated on the basis of colouration, into a peripheral sapwood and a central heartwood. Sapwood is physiologically active in the storage of reserve foods and in the movement of water and minerals from root to crown. Heartwood contains no living cells and is non-functional except for mechanical support.

Wood is composed of two interpenetrating systems of cells, one system oriented longitudinally and the second radially. Members of the axial or longitudinal system of cells, including vessel members, tracheids, fibres and parenchyma, are all derived from the fusiform initials. The radial system of cells, the rays, is derived from the ray initials of the vascular cambium and is totally parenchymatous, except in some softwoods, e.g. pine, wherein ray tracheids occur.

Softwoods are structurally homogeneous in that about 90% of the axial elements are tracheids. Hardwoods are by contrast more heterogeneous containing vessel members, fibres and sometimes (e.g. oak) tracheids. In addition to dissimilarity in cellular composition, the softwoods and hardwoods show interesting differences in the development of certain axial cells. Tracheids of softwoods are about 3–4.0 mm in length whereas fibres of hardwoods are much shorter, a length of 1–1.5 mm being most common. Differences are apparent not only in the final dimensions but also in the development of these elements from their fusiform initials. The mature fibre is up to × 5 longer than the fusiform initial from which it arose. By contrast, tracheids show only slight increase, 20–30%, in length over their initials. It might be asked why fibres elongate so extensively during differentiation. The ultimate answer is to be found in the interaction of the genetic potential of the differentiating cell and the sequence of environmental changes, mostly physiological, encountered in the vicinity of the vascular cambium.

To some extent during the normal course of tree growth changes occur in the development of fibres and tracheids indicating that genetic control is not so rigid as to prevent the occurrence of variation. Long ago Bailey (see references in ESAU, 1965) observed that structural variability of wood elements exists not only on a generic and species level, but even within the organism itself. Thus, within a single annual ring of a softwood there is variation of tracheid length based on position, e.g. between trunkwood and branchwood. Where branches are inserted on the trunk, tracheids are shorter than those immediately above or below. Even at a given level in a tree trunk there is a gradual increase in tracheid length from the first to

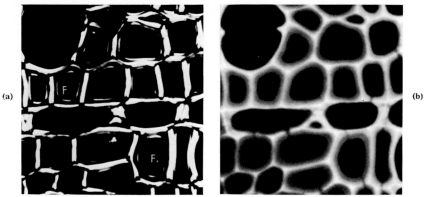

(a)

(b)

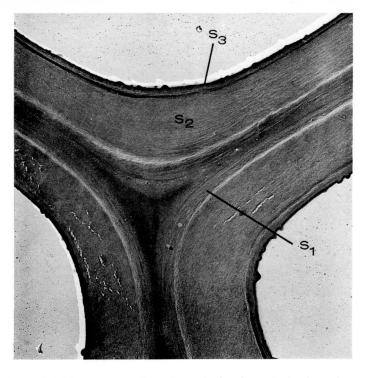

(c)

Plate 1 (**a**) Transverse section of wood of red maple in the polarizing microscope. In each fibre (F) two zones of optical anisotropy are observed, an outer bright zone corresponding to the primary wall plus the S_1 layer, and a thin inner zone, the S_3 layer. In this orientation the S_2 layer is dark. (**b**) Photomicrograph showing fluorescence caused by lignin in the same section. The distribution of lignin in the cell wall may be measured by the characteristic blue or blue-green fluorescence emitted in response to absorption of ultraviolet light. In wood fibres the lignin content is high in the middle lamella and primary wall. (Photographs from Figs. 2 and 4, p. 291 of MOREY and CRONSHAW, 1968.) (**c**) Transverse section of tracheids of *Pinus pungens* (table-mountain pine) showing the S_1, S_2 and S_3 layers of the secondary wall. (Electron micrograph courtesy of W. A. Côté, Jr., from Fig. 4, p. 13 of CÔTÉ and DAY, 1969.)

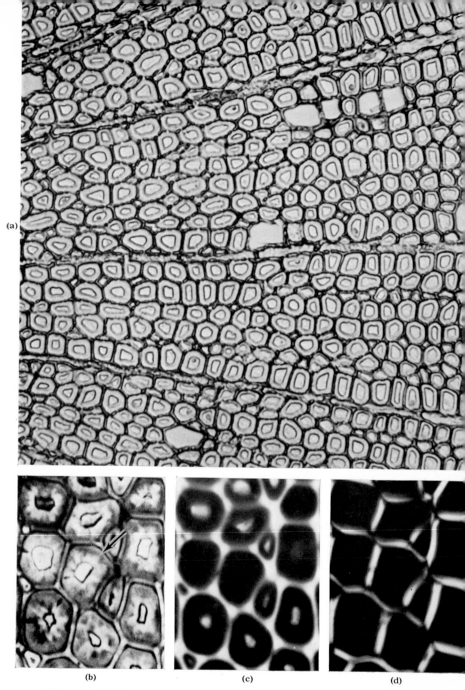

Plate 2 (a),(b) Transverse section of tension wood from red maple. The thick S(G) layer (arrow) of tension wood fibres is prominent. (c),(d) Same section as in (b) but in the fluorescence and polarization microscopes respectively. (c) The absence of fluorescence in the S(G) layer indicates a low lignin content. (d) The same layer shows little or no birefringence, an indication of the axial alignment of cellulose (§2.2).

about the sixtieth annual ring. Thereafter this dimension remains more or less constant.

2.2   Chemical composition

The structure of wood and many of its properties are based on the characteristic arrangement of the component cells. The even wear of maple furniture results from a relatively uniform distribution of vessel members and fibres in the wood of each annual ring. On the other hand, the fine furrows eventually developed in tables and chairs made of oak, not an altogether unpleasant property, is caused by the localized occurrence of very wide vessel members in the earliest portion of each annual ring. The structure of wood may, however, be understood not only in terms of the arrangement of

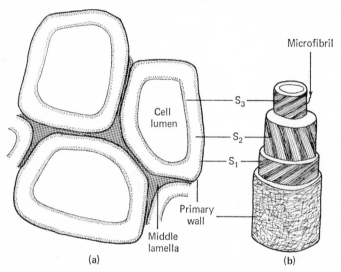

Fig. 2–2   Drawing showing organization of the cell wall of wood fibres. By means of polarized light and electron microscopy, wall layers are distinguished on the basis of the differing alignment of their microfibrils.

its cells, but also, and more fundamentally, on the basis of the organization and chemistry of the cell wall substance.

Fibres and tracheids are characterized by cell walls heterogeneous in both structure and chemical composition. *Primary cell wall* is the term applied to the original cambial wall. The primary cell wall is capable of growing in surface area as, e.g. when a vessel member increases in diameter. Adjacent cambial derivatives are, at this early stage of differentiation, separated only by two thin primary walls joined by an intercellular substance called the *middle lamella*. In mature tracheids and fibres however, the primary cell wall, now the outermost portion of the cell wall (Fig. 2–2), accounts for only a small percentage of the wall substance. A thick *secondary cell wall* is deposited on the inner side of the primary cell wall soon after the latter ceases to undergo surface growth. The secondary cell wall contains by far the majority of the cell wall substance. Primary and secondary cell walls are composed of three major constituents, cellulose and hemicellulose, both polysaccharides, and lignin, an aromatic polymer derived from phenyl-propane building blocks (C_6–C_3 units, see Fig. 2–4). Cellulose may be likened to a framework material giving form and structure to the cell wall (WARDROP, 1964a). Cellulose is initially embedded in a porous, amorphous, matrix of hemicellulose. Later on, these polysaccharides are encrusted, and thereby cemented together, with lignin which is a very stable, three-dimensional polymer.

2.2.1   Cellulose   The most abundant naturally occurring organic substance, *cellulose*, was recognized long ago as the major constituent of the plant cell wall and for this reason was so named. The physical organization of the cell wall is based on cellulose. The molecule is long and straight, consisting of several thousand glucose units linked end to end. Cellulose molecules, in numbers up to 2000 are aligned in parallel array into threads known as *microfibrils* (Fig. 2–2). Several hundred microfibrils, may be aligned together in discrete units known as *macrofibrils*, visible in the light microscope as fine striations in the cell wall. Macrofibrils are organized laterally as *lamellae* and a number of these in turn compose a cell wall *layer*. In wood fibres the secondary cell wall consists of three distinct layers, named from the outside toward the cell lumen, as S_1, S_2, and S_3 respectively (Plate 1c). The arrangement of cellulose molecules in the cell wall is thus one of increasing order of complexity, from the microfibrils visible only in electron micrographs, through the macrofibrils, lamellae and layers, that ultimately comprise the secondary cell wall of macroscopic dimension.

Cellulose alone among the principal cell wall constituents is partially crystalline. Cellulose molecules, in regions of the microfibrils, known as *micelles*, are aligned in a very regular manner forming a crystal lattice. The molecules which comprise the lattice have different arrangements along different axes; cellulose is *anisotropic* (ESAU, 1965). On the basis of this property, cellulose can readily be detected in a polarizing microscope. In this instrument polaroid filters are inserted in the optic axis, one just below the condenser and a second in the body tube. When both filters are similarly oriented, plane polarized light, that is light vibrating in only one plane, issues from the first filter, known as the *polarizer*, and passes unchanged through the second filter, the *analyzer*. If the analyzer is now rotated 90 degrees with respect to the polarizer no light is passed; plane polarized light is extinguished and the field as seen through the ocular is dark.

Cellulose contains two planes of polarization; it is *optically anisotropic*. Polarized light impinging on cellulose, from any oblique angle, is resolved into two components vibrating in these planes. The component vibrations become out of phase, and do not recombine to give the original beam. They are passed by the analyzer and the specimen appears bright in an otherwise dark field. The optical anisotropy of cellulose is most evident when polarized light impinges at right angles to the long axis of the cellulose chain. Optical anisotropy, however, is not evident when the plane of polarization of the incident beam is parallel to one of the two planes of polarization of cellulose. For example, a portion of a fibre cell wall may remain dark between crossed polaroids, if the cellulose chains, and consequently one of its planes of polarization, are oriented parallel to the optic axis of the microscope, that is, parallel to plane of vibration of incident polarized light.

The polarizing microscope can be used to detect and determine the orientation of cellulose in fibres and tracheids since this is the only cell wall component that is optically anisotropic. Thus, in transverse section between crossed polaroids, the S_2 layer shows very little optical anisotropy (Plate 1a). In longitudinal section however, when the same layer is laid out flat on the microscope stage, anisotropy is fully expressed; the S_2 layer is bright. Obviously then, the cellulose chains in the S_2 layer are oriented in a predominant axial direction at only a slight angle to the long cell axis. Measurements with the polarization and electron microscopes show that this angle is 10–30 degrees for fibres and tracheids (see ROELOFSEN, 1959). The S_1 and S_3 layers are generally bright in transverse section between crossed polaroids (Plate 1a). Cellulose in these layers is aligned at angles of 60–90 degrees to fibre and tracheid axis (Fig. 2–2b).

The thick secondary wall of woody plant cells is heterogeneous in terms of organization of its framework substance. The strength of wood is based, in part, on this laminated structure, which may be likened to plyboard, the subunits of which though inherently weak are bound together to form a very strong aggregate.

2.2.2 Hemicellulose   Cellulose accounts for only slightly more than half of the polysaccharide found in the woody plant cell wall. The other major group of cell wall polysaccharides, the *hemicelluloses* are a very diverse, distinct group of low molecular weight polymers. They are insoluble in water, like cellulose, and extractable in aqueous alkali, unlike cellulose. Although hemicelluloses are essentially linear molecules, they may be variously branched providing the porous matrix found around the cellulose microfibrils.

Some striking differences occur between angiosperms and gymnosperms in terms of the gross chemical composition of wood. The hemicelluloses of hardwoods are usually present in greater amounts than those of softwoods. On the other hand, more lignin is present in the wood of softwoods than hardwoods. It is interesting to note that among the major constituents of wood, cellulose is the only one that exhibits relative constancy, values of 40–45% being common for hardwoods and softwoods alike. Some variations in the properties of softwoods and hardwoods are understood on the basis of gross differences in the chemical composition of the wood. Given similar environmental conditions, the wood of an angiosperm usually contains more moisture than that of a conifer. Hemicellulose is the most hygroscopic of the major cell wall constituents (ROELOFSEN, 1959) and, this being so, the higher moisture content of hardwoods derives from the relatively greater amount of this wood constituent.

2.2.3   Lignin   In the final phase of differentiation of a wood tracheid or fibre, the cell wall is encrusted and made rigid by lignin. This is a highly aromatic substance, and the only major non-carbohydrate of the cell wall. The basic building blocks of lignin are phenylpropane units, linked together in various ways, e.g. by carbon to carbon and ether linkages. In softwoods coniferyl alcohol is the predominant building block of lignin whereas in hardwoods (Fig. 2–4) sinapyl and coniferyl alcohol units are utilized in equal amounts. These units are dehydrogenated and subsequently constructed into a complex three-dimensional polymer that completely encrusts the polysaccharide wall components.

Lignin is a stable, rigid polymer. One procedure used to isolate solid lignin from wood is incubation in strong mineral acid, for example 72% (w/w) sulphuric acid, a reagent which readily hydrolyzes cell wall polysaccharide. Softwoods tracheids placed in sulphuric acid retain to a high degree their original morphology indicating the stabilizing effect of lignin in the cell wall. In peat bogs the percentage of lignin in the plant debris, generally increases with depth illustrating the relative inertness of lignin among the major cell wall constituents.

Wood chemists have, for many years, been interested in the amount of lignin in the cell wall layers of tracheids and fibres. Knowledge of the distribution of lignin is important in chemical pulping where lignin is extracted and wood is broken down into its cellular elements.

Lignin absorbs light very strongly in the ultraviolet band with characteristic maxima at 212 and 280 nanometres (Plate 1b). The concentration of lignin at any point in the cell wall can be related specifically to the *absorption* of ultraviolet light. Using 0.5-micron-thick sections of wood of black spruce and a monochromatic light source (280 nm), SCOTT et al. (1969) recorded the absorbance of ultraviolet light by lignin photomicrographically with an ultraviolet microscope (Fig. 2–3a). This instrument is basically similar to the conventional microscope with the exception that glass optics are replaced with those of quartz which transmits ultraviolet light. A microdensitometer then records the ultraviolet absorbance along a straight line trace across the tracheid wall (Fig. 2–3b).

The relative absorbance due to lignin in the primary wall and middle lamella is much higher than in the secondary wall. Calculations show that the *lignin content* of the primary wall and middle lamella in early wood tracheids is 0.50 and 0.85 (g/g) respectively (FERGUS et al., 1969). In the secondary wall a much lower, uniform, concentration of 0.23 (g/g) is calculated. It should be recalled at this point that the secondary cell wall is the most conspicuous wall layer of fibres and tracheids (Fig. 2–2). In black spruce it accounts for 87% of the wall volume of early wood tracheids

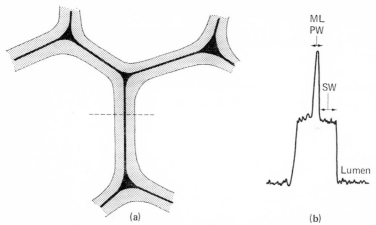

ML
PW

SW

Lumen

(a)   (b)

Fig. 2–3 (a) Drawing showing the distribution of lignin across tracheid cell walls recorded photomicrographically by absorbance of ultraviolet light. (b) Microdensitometer trace revealing high absorbance in the middle lamella (ML) and primary wall (PW) and a somewhat lesser, but even, absorbance across the secondary wall (SW). (Based on Figs. 1 and 2, pp. 76, 77, from SCOTT et al., 1969.)

(FERGUS et al., 1969). If the distribution of lignin is now calculated on the basis of percentage of *total lignin*, the secondary cell wall is found to contain 72% of the total with lesser amounts in the primary wall and middle lamella respectively. Thus, in spite of a relatively low lignin content, the bulk of the total wood lignin occurs in the thick secondary cell wall.

2.3   Formation of the cell wall

Tracheids, vessel members, fibres, axial and ray parenchyma cells, all differentiate from cambial initials along a developmental pathway having four somewhat overlapping steps: (1) cell division, (2) surface growth, (3) wall thickening and (4) lignification (WARDROP, 1964a).

The *division* of fusiform and ray initials in the tangential plane produces both secondary xylem and phloem and also accounts for the predominant arrangement of the differentiated cells in radial rows. As the woody cylinder enlarges, the vascular cambium increases in circumference. This is accomplished by division in the radial plane leading to an increased number of cambial initials.

The primary cell wall of cambial derivatives undergoes *surface growth* during differentiation. Hardwood fibres grow predominately in the longitudinal direction becoming up to × 5 the length of the initial from which they arose. During *cell wall thickening* the three-layered secondary cell wall is formed. The reader should bear in mind that surface growth and cell wall thickening are not mutually exclusive and may, in fact, occur at the same time. For example, fibres grow by surface growth at their tips, while at the same time, the secondary cell wall is being deposited in the more proximal portion of the cell.

The final step in the differentiation of the fibre and tracheid cell wall is lignification. Recent biochemical work shows that the lignin precursor arises in the lignifying cell itself. A critical step in lignin biosynthesis is the

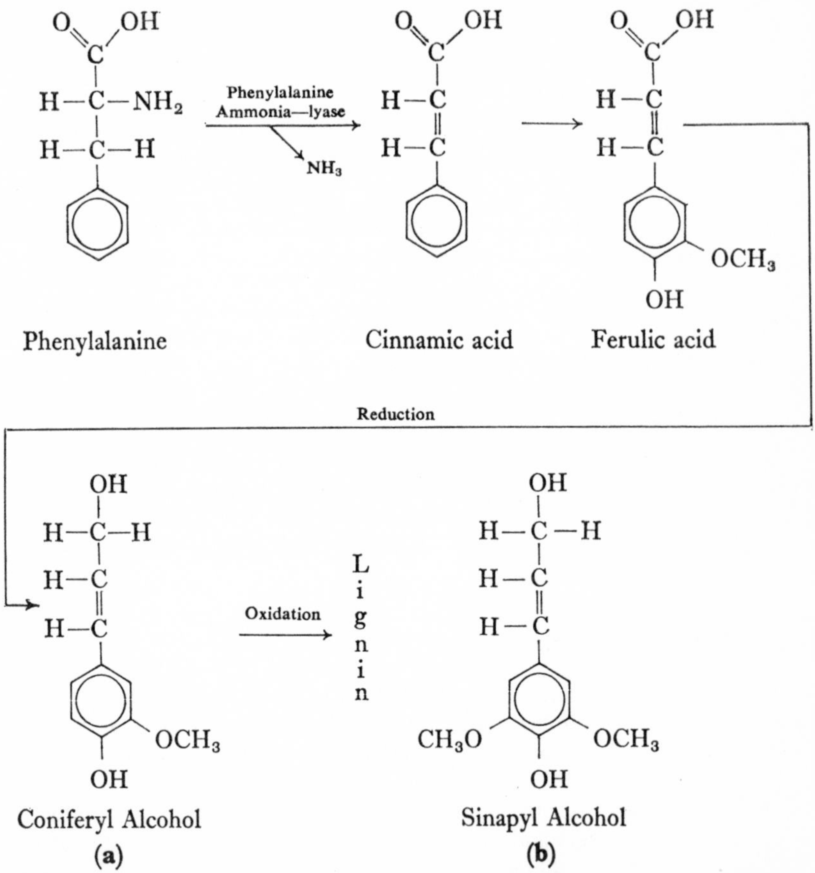

Fig. 2-4   (a) Scheme showing derivation of the lignin precursor, coniferyl alcohol in gymnosperms, from phenylalanine. (b) In angiosperms both coniferyl and sinapyl alcohols function as lignin precursors.

deamination of L-phenylalanine by phenylalanine ammonia-lyase (Fig. 2–4). Cinnamic acid, the product, is converted along a pathway ending with coniferyl alcohol. Coniferyl alcohol and related alcohols are dehydrogenated by oxidative enzymes, e.g. peroxidase, and converted to lignin. By means of a simple dissection technique, RUBERY and NORTHCOTE (1968) separated differentiating xylem tissue, in which lignin synthesis is high, from the cambial zone where little lignin is formed. Differentiating xylem showed high phenylalanine ammonia-lyase activity, whereas little enzyme was present in the cambial zone. Furthermore, the excised differentiating cells readily incorporate tritiated cinnamic acid into lignin whereas little incorporation occurs in the cambial zone. Differentiating cambial derivatives make their own lignin precursors, and these are directly incorporated into cell wall lignin. Lignification then, is not dependent on a supply of precursors from the cambial region.

Radial Growth

3.1 The vascular cambium

Whereas height growth is associated with the organogenetic activities of the apical meristem and internode extension (Chapter 1), radial growth results from the activities of the cells of the vascular cambium. Perhaps the most characteristic step in radial growth is the *periclinal* division (division in the tangential plane) of cambial cells giving rise to rows of radially aligned elements of the wood and phloem. This brings about a gradual outward displacement of the meristem itself as its inner derivative cells differentiate and the woody core grows by accretion.

Observation of a cross section of a woody stem in the spring reveals several layers of actively dividing cambial cells and, in addition, a continuum of cells both to the inside and outside differentiating respectively as xylem and phloem elements. Those cells of the vascular cambium undergoing division comprise the *cambial zone*. From this position inward xylem elements are differentiating in a regular manner along the developmental pathway of surface growth, wall thickening and lignification. On the basis of structural characteristics certain cells of the cambial zone may be interpreted as the *cambial initials* (PHILIPSON et al., 1971). Periclinal division here results in the formation of one daughter initial maintaining the continuum of the meristem, and second cell cut off toward the inside or outside which eventually gives rise to xylem or phloem respectively. Other cells of the cambial zone to the inside and outside of the cambial initials are interpreted as *xylem mother* and *phloem mother cells* respectively. Division of a mother cell in the periclinal plane produces two derivatives *both* of which later develop into xylem or phloem elements.

Periclinal division in the elongate cells of the cambial zone necessarily entails the formation of a partition wall over a considerable distance, a process which has fascinated botanists for many years. Cell division may arbitrarily be separated into two phases: (1) *mitosis* or division of the nuclear material and (2) *cytokinesis* involving partitioning of cytoplasm between daughter cells (ESAU, 1965). In most plant cells the entire process of cell division is completed rapidly, but in elongate periclinally dividing cambial cells cytokinesis is considerably extended both in time and space. In the anaphase stage of mitosis, two groups of daughter chromosomes move away from the equatorial plane, along a fibrous spindle termed the phragmoplast. During telophase a partition wall, the *cell plate*, begins to form between the dividing protoplasts in the central zone of the equatorial plane. At first, the cell plate consists of the limiting cell membrane of the daughter protoplasts together with a common middle lamella. Later on a cellulosic primary wall is secreted by each daughter cell. Toward the end of telophase the phragmoplast comes to occupy a peripheral position at the rim, around and just in front of the growing, disc-like cell plate. The cell plate continues to extend so that it shortly reaches the radial walls of the dividing cell. Now the phragmoplast consists of two separate portions, each growing in opposite directions just ahead of the cell plate as the latter extends to the far ends of the periclinally dividing call (Fig. 3–1). This process occurs with such regularity that radial rows of xylem elements are formed, e.g., the tracheids of softwoods.

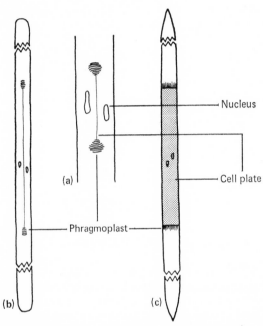

Fig. 3–1   Periclinal division of a fusiform initial. The phragmoplast is just ahead of the advancing edge of the cell plate. Radial longitudinal sections showing (a) early and (b) later stages of phragmoplast and cell plate development in sectional view. (c) Tangential longitudinal section with new partition wall in surface view. (Redrawn from Figs. 10–12, Plate I, BAILEY, 1920.)

Comparison of a one or two-year-old twig with a 100-year-old branch shows that growth in diameter also involves a considerable increase in the circumference of the cambial initial layer. Although, during ontogeny, the cambial initials do expand tangentially (Table 1, p. 23, GEMMELL, 1969), this alone falls far short of accounting for the increasing girth of the vascular cambium. Cell divisions therefore must occur perpendicular to the surface of woody stems and branches and these divisions, termed *anti-clinal*, are largely responsible for the maintenance of the lateral continuity of the vascular cambium during radial growth. Anticlinal division is usually restricted to the cambial initials. Two types of anticlinal division are dis-tinguished, based on the inclination of the partition wall formed during cytokinesis. In gymnosperms and some angiosperms (e.g. walnuts) *pseudotransverse* anticlinal division occurs wherein the partition wall is obliquely oriented with respect to the long axis of the cell (Fig. 3–2a). Fusiform initials dividing in this manner give rise to two daughter cells both of which are initially shorter than the parent cell. Increase in circum-ference is then accomplished through a mechanism combining (1) apical extension growth of each daughter cell, so that the total number of initials present in any transverse plane increases, and (2) lateral expansion following

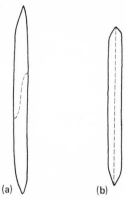

(a)   (b)

Fig. 3–2   Tangential longitudinal view of fusiform initials showing **(a)** pseudotransverse and **(b)** radial anticlinal divisions.

division. In other angiosperms (*Robinia*) anticlinal division is *radial longitudinal*, that is, the partition wall traverses the fusiform initial from top to bottom in the radial plane (Fig. 3–2b). The daughter initials are the same height as the parent cell and furthermore they usually show little or no tendency toward apical extension. Increase in circumference, in trees with radial longitudinal division, is accomplished simply by tangential expansion of the daughter initials.

3.2   Seasonal development

Recently there has been considerable investigation of the sequence of developmental events occurring in the vascular cambium of trees of the temperate latitudes. The following account, given in a descriptive manner only, is of the seasonal course of periclinal division leading to the produc-tion of new xylem and phloem in the vascular cambium of representative gymnosperms and angiosperms.

In white cedar (*Thuja occidentalis*) the period of xylem differentiation begins (Ontario, Canada) before that of the phloem. The overwintering cambial zone consists of only 3 layers of cells, with a single outer layer of cambial initials and two layers of xylem mother cells (Fig. 3–3a; BANNAN, 1962). In mid-April, the first periclinal divisions are observed in the cambial zone in the xylem mother cells (Fig. 3–3b). During May there is a high frequency of division in these cells, so that by the end of the month the cambial zone is wide and the innermost derivatives are rapidly differentiating as tracheids (Fig. 3–3c). At the same time the cambial initials occasionally divide giving rise to new xylem and phloem mother cells. The latter divide once and then the derivatives differentiate into elements of the phloem.

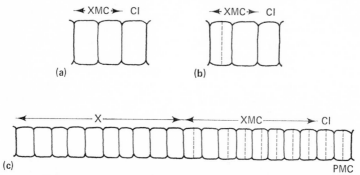

Fig. 3–3 Diagram showing the usual sequence of initiation of cambial activity in white cedar. See text for explanation. CI = cambial initial. XMC = xylem mother cell. PMC = phloem mother cell. X = differentiating xylem cell. (After BANNAN, 1962, Fig. 1–1a, 1–1b, 1–1h, p. 5. Adapted from *Tree Growth*, edited by THEODORE KOZLOWSKI, copyright © 1962, The Ronald Press Company, New York.)

By the end of May there are, on average, only 2 phloem elements while on the other side of the cambial initials there are up to 60 cells in various stages of development.

Recent investigations show that the pattern of seasonal activity in the pines differs markedly from white cedar. In eastern white pine (*Pinus strobus*), the differentiation of cells of the phloem (Wisconsin, Central USA) begins up to 6 weeks before that of the xylem (ALFIERI and EVERT, 1968). At the end of March phloem formation begins with the differentiation of sieve cells directly from the outermost cells of the cambial zone without any preceding cell division. Although periclinal division occurs slowly in the cambial zone in April, it is not until early May that xylem mother cells differentiate as tracheids. A strong surge of xylem development follows from mid-May to mid-June and this is accomplished by means of a high rate of periclinal division of xylem mother cells and the rapid maturation of the derivative cells. Alfieri and Evert report, in addition, that the last formed sieve cells of the autumn overwinter and remain functional for the first part of the following growing season.

The seasonal cycle of cambial activity in angiosperms may conveniently be divided into two patterns based on the size and distribution of vessels which occur in the xylem of the annual ring. In some trees with *diffuse porous* wood (*Acer*), where vessels of similar size are distributed uniformly throughout the annual ring, the differentiation of phloem precedes that of xylem by 4 to 6 weeks. On the other hand in some ring porous trees (*Robinia*), where the largest vessels occur only in the earliest part of the annual increment, xylem and phloem develop more or less simultaneously.

In diffuse porous *Acer negundo* (box elder) sieve tube members, differentiated in the previous autumn, overwinter and remain functional during the following spring (TUCKER and EVERT, 1969). Cambial activity begins in late March (Wisconsin) with the differentiation of cells from the outer face of the cambial zone directly into phloem elements. At the same time the remaining layers of the cambial zone, especially those on the phloem side, begin to undergo periclinal division. Only much later, in mid-May, do the first xylem elements mature. In many respects then the cycle of cambial activity in *Acer* is similar to that of pine since in both cases (1) functional sieve elements are present on a year round basis, (2) the formation of new phloem occurs about a month before that of the xylem and (3) new phloem elements arise in the early spring directly from the outermost undifferentiated cells of the cambial zone.

In mid-April (Wisconsin) in ring porous *Robinia pseudoacacia* (black locust) periclinal division occurs in the outer cells of the cambial zone and phloem elements are rapidly differentiated (DERR and EVERT, 1967). Also, at the same time, periclinal division begins to occur in the rest of the cambial zone. However, differentiating xylem elements mature slowly and several rows of sieve tube members are produced before the first vessel members. This bewildering variation in timing of phloem and xylem production in angiosperms and gymnosperms may be understood in terms of a unifying hormonal thesis (see § 3.4).

3.3   Initiation of cambial activity

Differences are apparent between ring and diffuse porous trees not only in the onset of xylem and phloem production, but also in the sequence of initiation of cambial activity at different positions in the trunk and branches. Consider the observations of HANSON and BRENKE (1926) on *Fraxinus campestris* (ring porous) and *Acer saccharinum* (diffuse porous) growing in sites near Lincoln, Nebraska (Central USA). Activity in the cambial zone of ash begins in mid-April and by April 27th it is observed that a similar amount of new wood is present in the lower trunk as well as in one-year-old branches. This suggests that the vascular cambium becomes active simultaneously throughout its vertical extent. It is observed also that periclinal division in the cambial zone begins just before the opening of the terminal buds. Obviously in ash a great amount of shoot growth is not essential to the stimulation of activity in the cambial zone.

On the other hand in maple, the terminal buds open in mid-April, yet xylem formation in the lower trunk lags for one or two weeks. On April 27th when shoot growth is well underway and the leaves are half their mature size, cambial activity is just being initiated in the trunk at the one foot level. However, at higher positions on the trunk (2.4 and 5.4 metres) the vascular cambium has been active for some time as evidenced by the presence of vessel members and fibres undergoing surface growth and wall thickening. In one-year-old twigs of the same tree the new xylem contains thick-walled vessel members which are partially lignified. In diffuse porous species, like maple, it appears that a wave of cambial activity progresses downward *slowly* from the uppermost twigs into the trunk.

More recent work with diffuse porous trees indicates a close relationship between the initiation of cambial activity and the production of auxin during shoot growth. This is well illustrated by comparison of cambial activity between completely disbudded and intact trees of *Acer pseudo-platanus* (sycamore maple). As expected, cambial activity in the intact trees is initiated in the twigs and progresses downward slowly so that by the end of May (London, Great Britain) radial growth is progressing rapidly throughout the length of the trunk (WAREING, 1951). However, in trees from which all branches, twigs and adventitious buds are removed, the vascular cambium remains inactive and no new xylem is produced. The only exception occurs when adventitious buds grow out from the trunk, and here cambial activity is limited strictly to a localized area beneath the insertion point of the bud. In diffuse porous trees shoot growth, when it occurs in *considerable amounts*, exercises control over the initiation of cambial activity and it is suggested that auxin is the mediating factor.

DIGBY and WAREING (1966b) recently examined the levels of auxin extractable at various heights from the cambial zone of the trunk of *Populus trichocarpa* (a diffuse porous tree) before, during and after bud break. Auxin is not extractable from the cambial zone at any height before bud break. However, during bud break considerable auxin is present in the upper part of the trunk, nearest the extending shoots, whereas little or none occurs at lower positions. Three weeks after bud break, when cambial activity is well established throughout the trunk, the level of auxin is uniformly high at all heights. Thus, in diffuse porous trees the slow basipetal pattern of cambial activation in the spring is associated with a downward flow of auxin produced in extending internodes and leaves of the crown.

By contrast the initiation of cambial activity in ring porous trees is more subtly controlled. For example, in debudded and intact *Fraxinus excelsior* WAREING (1951) finds that cambial activity in both cases is initiated at the same time throughout the trunk and, furthermore, that the new increment of xylem in both instances contains wide vessels. This suggests that cambial activity in ring porous trees is stimulated by very low levels of auxin (in debudded trees perhaps produced from minute buds associated with leaf scars) or that an auxin precursor, already present in the vascular cambium, is activated simultaneously throughout the trunk and branches.

In ring porous trees, buds, even when very minute, exert control over cambial activity. When dormant stem segments of ash are brought into a warm laboratory, the vascular cambium becomes active especially at the basal end (WAREING, 1951). If the bark is stripped away, new, wide vessels are always traceable up to (but not above) the former position of a small bud (Fig. 3–4). This leads to greater radial growth at the lower end of the stem segment. Although we cannot be sure as to their exact role, this observation makes it clear that buds, even of very small size, are involved in the control of incipient cambial activity in ring porous species.

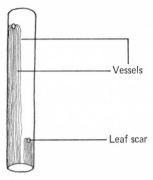

Fig. 3–4 Diagram showing the distribution of new vessels in stem segment of ash. Vessels differentiate in relation to small adventitious buds formed at old leaf scars. (After Fig. 4, p. 555, WAREING, 1951.)

Recent work shows that the simultaneous onset of cambial activity in ring porous *Ulmus glabra* is explicable in terms of the activation of an auxin precursor (DIGBY and WAREING, 1966b). In February, high levels of a growth stimulator, most probably tryptophan, are present in the cambial zone at all heights in the trunk. At the time of bud swelling tryptophan is converted to indole-3-acetic acid (IAA) and cambial activity is simultaneously initiated throughout the trunk. The role of buds, and perhaps other factors, in regulating the conversion of tryptophan to IAA remains for future work.

3.4 Hormonal control of xylem and phloem formation

In addition to the initiation of cambial activity auxin is involved in the differentiation of cambial derivatives. This is shown in experiments in which IAA and gibberellic acid (GA) are applied, in a lanolin carrier separately or together, to dormant debudded stems of *Acer pseudoplatanus* (WAREING, 1958). Examination of sections cut from stems 1–3 weeks later shows that lanolin alone is without effect; the vascular cambium remains inactive. However, in response to IAA, a thin zone of xylem is formed containing lignified vessel members, but no mature fibres. GA alone promotes some cell division but, unlike IAA, there is no further differentiation of the cambial derivatives. When both hormones are applied together a wide increment of xylem resembling normal wood develops. The wood contains lignified fibres and vessel members. Both auxin and gibberellin then are involved in the normal development of the secondary xylem. However, the roles of the hormones are distinct in that auxin is primarily involved in the differentiation of cambial derivatives while gibberellin stimulates cell division leading to the production of the cambial derivatives.

Whereas the differentiation of xylem is promoted by auxin, recent work shows that a high level of gibberellin brings about phloem formation (DIGBY and WAREING, 1966a). Application of GA to stems of debudded, non-dormant *Populus robusta* causes the formation of a thick increment of phloem. At the same time, GA shows no effect on xylem differentiation. When IAA is applied alone xylem differentiation is promoted but there is an absence of phloem formation. These experiments suggest that xylem production is favoured by a high ratio of applied auxin/gibberellin, whereas a high gibberellin content promotes phloem differentiation.

There is some indication that the seasonal timing of xylem and phloem production may be explicable in terms of a changing balance of auxin and gibberellin in the vascular cambium. In this regard, DIGBY and WAREING (1966b) measured the auxin and gibberellin contents in stems and leaves of *Ailanthus altissima* (a ring porous tree) grown under long day conditions and then transferred to a short day regime. Although xylem formation ceases three weeks after transfer to short days, the stem diameter continues to increase as new phloem is formed for an additional two weeks. Under long days a high level of both auxin and gibberellin occurs in stems and leaves, but after transfer to a short photoperiod the auxin content drops and 4 weeks later very little auxin is detectable. It is at this time that xylem is no longer being differentiated. By contrast, the gibberellin level remains high even after 4 weeks of short day treatment and phloem alone is being produced. These experiments suggest that *endogenous* levels of auxin and gibberellin are operative in controlling the formation of xylem and phloem. Further work may show that the timing of xylem and phloem production in gymnosperms and angiosperms (§ 3.2) is explicable in terms of a changing seasonal balance of growth substances in the cambial zone.

The work of WAREING (1958) on *Acer pseudoplatanus* shows that auxin and gibberellin act together in promoting normal xylem development. In addition, there is evidence that developmental processes in the vascular cambium involve the interaction of other factors. For example, in stem segments of crack willow (*Salix fragilis*), ROBARDS et al. (1969) discovered that the number of cells in the differentiating xylem undergoing extensive growth in width (presumptive vessel members) is increased by separate application for an array of substances including auxins, GA, 6-furfury-

Table 1 Effect of chemicals on xylem differentiation in stem segments of willow. FAP = 6-furfurylaminopurine; SUC = sucrose; INO = myo-inositol. (From p. 915 of Short-term Effects of some Chemicals on Cambial Activity by A. W. ROBARDS, E. DAVIDSON and P. KIDWAI, 1969. By permission of the Clarendon Press, Oxford.)

Treatment	Percentage of vessel members among differentiating xylem cells
Control	2.8 ± 0.6
IAA	9.6 ± 0.5
GA	9.2 ± 1.1
FAP	7.2 ± 0.5
SUC	12.6 ± 0.8
INO	13.1 ± 1.7
IAA + GA + FAP + SUC	31.5 ± 4.7

laminopurine (a cytokinin), sucrose and myo-inositol (Table 1). When these chemicals are applied together there is a large increase in the number of vessel members over and above that brought about by any substance alone. ROBARDS et al. (1969) point out that we should not be too quick in attributing an aspect of differentiation causally to a single substance when, in fact, an array of substances might interact endogenously.

3.5 Physiology of annual ring formation

Careful observation of a thin transverse section of wood from trees of the temperate latitudes shows that there is an obvious structural dissimilarity between the xylem formed at different times during the growing season. In gymnosperms, the tracheids of the earliest-formed wood have a greater radial diameter and a thinner secondary cell wall than those differentiated later in the season (see plate 4, GEMMELL, 1969). Likewise in ring porous angiosperms there is a decrease in vessel diameter from the beginning to the end of the yearly xylem increment. The terms *early wood* and *late wood* are used respectively to distinguish between the initially less dense and the subsequently more dense wood formed during the sequence of radial growth. The structural dissimilarity between the late wood of one season and the early wood of the next year is the basis for the recognition of the periodic nature of wood production as seen clearly by the occurrence of the *annual ring*. This term refers to the xylem increment, including both early and late wood, produced during a single annual growth cycle. In the branches and trunks of some trees however, the annual xylem increment may contain two *growth rings*, as for example when radial growth is temporarily interrupted by a severe summer drought. The second growth ring is referred to as a *false annual ring* (ESAU, 1965).

The transition from early to late wood is associated with two experimentally separable, but usually coincident, aspects of xylem cell differ-

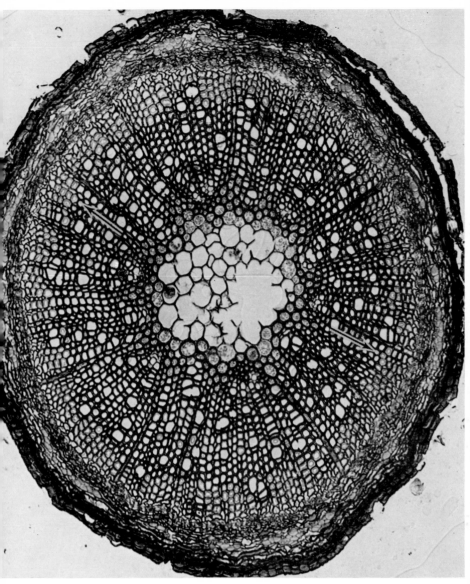

Plate 3 Transverse section from a stem of an eight-week-old maple seedling which had been treated two weeks previously with TIBA (in lanolin) applied as a ring around the midpoint of the first internode. The section was cut from the erect stem about 1.0 mm below the treatment site. A complete ring of tension wood was differentiated during experimental treatment. Note the tension wood fibres (arrows). (After Fig. 19, p. 299, MOREY and CRONSHAW, 1968.)

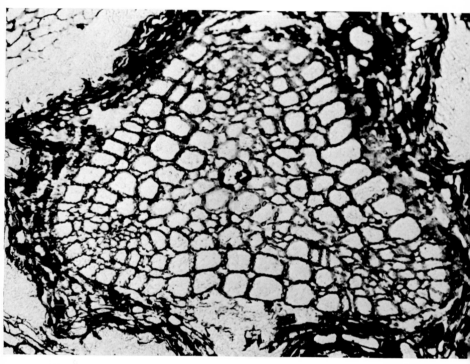

Plate 4 Transverse section of stem of *Sphenophyllum*. The secondary xylem initially shows a triangular arrangement reflecting the organization of the primary xylem. Later on a cylindrical woody core develops. (Photomicrograph courtesy of E. D. MOREY.)

entiation, namely decreasing cell size and increasing cell wall thickness. Late wood formation begins at the base of the trunk and progresses steadily upward into the branches. Thus, there is a higher proportion of late wood in the same annual ring near the base than higher up on the trunk.

The diameter growth of differentiating xylem cells during wood formation is thought to be controlled by the availability of auxin emanating from the shoot. It is known that environmental factors such as short photoperiods and drought which decrease the extension growth of the shoot, also hasten the formation of late wood in the subjacent trunk. Because extending leaves and internodes are rich sources of auxin (§ 1.3), it is suspected that auxin produced in the shoot mediates the diameter growth of differentiating xylem cells in the stem below. Strong supportive evidence is found in experiments on the effect of photoperiod on wood formation in young trees of *Pinus resinosa* (red pine). In trees grown under long days (18 hour photoperiod) early wood is formed and this is correlated with a high auxin content in the rapidly growing shoot (LARSON, 1962). Shoot growth and auxin content are both decreased by transfer for 2 weeks to short days (8 hour photoperiod) and late wood is now formed. Transfer of red pine from the short day regime back to long days causes renewed shoot growth, an increased auxin content and the deposition of a new increment of early wood. Here is an experimental situation in which a false growth ring is produced.

Direct evidence for the control of cell size by auxin is seen in experiments in which IAA is applied to decapitated stems of red pine growing under short days. Wide tracheids are induced in response to IAA instead of the narrow ones formed previously (LARSON, 1962). The normal acropetal progress of late wood formation is then explained by the decreasing availability of auxin, especially to the lower trunk, as shoot growth in the crown declines. Auxin is available at high concentrations and for a longer time at successively higher levels in the trunk and branches. Hence, the sequence of late wood formation, at least in terms of cell size, is acropetal.

A similar case is made for the regulation of vessel member diameter in ring porous *Robinia pseudoacacia* (DIGBY and WAREING, 1966a). When two-year-old seedlings are grown under short days for three weeks, shoot growth, cambial activity and xylem production all cease. Now if the shoot is decapitated and IAA in varying concentrations together with a constant low level of GA is applied to the decapitated stem cambial activity resumes and xylem is formed. In the experimentally induced xylem there is a clear correlation between vessel member diameter and the concentration of applied auxin. We may speculate then that the enlargement of differentiating vessel members is regulated by seasonally varying concentrations of endogenous auxin flowing from the crown.

Cell wall thickening in late wood formation is associated with the increased availability of products of photosynthesis as the foliage of the shoot matures. This relationship is clearly seen where the contribution of both one-year-old and newly emergent needles to shoot growth and wood formation is measured in red pine trees brought into a warm greenhouse (18 hour photoperiod) in December (GORDON and LARSON, 1968). Needles more than one-year-old, lateral buds and branches are all removed previously, in the autumn, to simplify the experimental system. From the third to the seventh week after bud break the new needles grow very rapidly, after which time elongation declines. During the third to the seventh week after bud break considerable photosynthate is exported from one-year-old needles upward into the terminal shoot where it is incorporated, for example, into the structural components of the new needle tissues. At the same time photosynthate is also being transported from one-year-old needles to other parts of the tree including the lower stem where thin-walled tracheids of the early wood are formed. During this time there is very little export of carbohydrate to other parts of the tree from the new needles themselves. Increase in cell wall thickness in differentiating tracheids of the lower stem occurs 7–9 weeks after bud break and this is correlated with the maturation of the new needles. Photosynthate is now transported out of the new needles and into the subjacent stem tissues. At the same time the photosynthate produced in the old needles, that is no longer needed for shoot growth above, is also available for incorporation into subjacent stem tissue. Thus, in red pine the transition from early to late wood appears causally associated with two events: (1) the sudden availability to the cambial zone of products of photosynthesis associated with the maturation of needles of the current-year-shoot and (2) a declining auxin level as extension growth in the crown ceases.

The concept that the transition from early to late wood is regulated simply by availability of auxin and photosynthate however, may be too simple. For example, many chemicals other than auxins and sugars affect the development of differentiating xylem cells (§ 3.4). In the final analysis then the regulation of annual ring formation may involve the wider interaction of gibberellins, cytokinins and growth inhibitors together with the established roles of auxin and photosynthate. The reader is referred to ZIMMERMANN and BROWN (1971) for a comprehensive treatment on the formation of growth rings.

3.6 Annual rings and climate

The formation of annual rings is affected indirectly by a whole array of environmental factors impinging on and thereby altering the growth of the tree crown. For example, when red pine is transferred from a long to short photoperiod shoot growth and auxin production decline and narrow cells characteristic of late wood are produced. Other environmental factors affecting wood formation include light intensity, temperature and defoliation (by insects or hail). In arid regions where drought is severe, available soil moisture can limit shoot growth and thereby lead to the development of a very narrow annual ring or no ring at all.

The influence of rainfall on the sequence of annual ring production is illustrated by comparison of tree growth on the California coast and in West Texas. In the vicinity of San Francisco, California most rain falls in the winter months. In the summer there is almost no rain at all. Soil moisture is highest in the early spring when tree growth begins, but thereafter falls with the absence of additional precipitation. The production of annual rings in trees growing in this region is very regular, there being only one period of radial growth of about the same intensity and duration each year (GLOCK and AGERTER, 1962). On the other hand, in Lubbock, Texas the growing season commences early in the spring when soil moisture is low. Although most rainfall occurs in the late spring and throughout the summer, precipitation is sporadic with periods of wetness separated by hot dry spells of variable duration. The sequence of growth rings formed under these conditions is most variable. The annual increment may in fact be a *multiple annual ring* in that several growth rings are formed each year. Other trees are characterized by partial growth rings, called *lenses*, in which the cambial zone fails to become active around the circumference of the trunk. Under conditions of exceptionally long drought, which sometimes occur in the American Southwest, soil moisture becomes insufficient to support tree growth and the annual ring is simply *missing* for that year. Obviously the task of determining the age of a large tree by counting annual rings is very difficult in West Texas, but somewhat easier in California.

By counting the sequence of annual rings it has recently been established that the bristlecone pines (*Pinus aristata*) of California are the world's oldest living trees. These trees grow very slowly at altitudes of 30–3300 metres in the arid White Mountains of California. An extreme example of the reduced rate of radial growth is seen in the occurrence of 1100 annual rings in a piece of wood 12.7 cm thick (FERGUSON, 1968).

A tree ring chronology, for example that of bristlecone pine, is built by determining in a relatively young tree the exact calendar year to which each annual ring corresponds. It is observed that the radial thickness of annual rings varies from year to year. Furthermore the same sequence is never repeated. Two specimens can be *cross dated* by careful inspection of the sequence of annual rings, for example by matching the positions of the most narrow rings. If a wood with an established history is cross dated with a slightly older wood containing a partially overlapping annual ring sequence, the chronology is extended further back in time. The oldest living bristlecone pine in the White Mountains is about 4600 years old, but by careful cross dating of wood from trees long dead, the chronology has recently been extended back through 7100 years (FERGUSON, 1968). Hopefully, the chronology can be continued for two additional millennia because bristlecone pine wood, about 9000 years old by radiocarbon analysis, has been found in the White Mountains.

Perhaps the most important aspect of tree ring chronology is that it provides a record of past regional climate. This is because the radial thickness of the annual ring is a good gauge of seasonal rainfall. Thus, a historical record of the past climate is preserved in the structure of the annual rings. In addition, the wood from the oldest dated trees is now being utilized as a standard for calibration of radiocarbon analysis so that archaeological artifacts from distant regions may be more accurately dated.

Reaction Wood 4

4.1 Structure and distribution of reaction wood

If a tree is displaced from the erect position a gradual reorientation occurs which is associated with the formation of wood of atypical structure and chemical composition. This wood, *reaction wood*, forms unilaterally along one or the other side of the displaced stem, and expands or contracts longitudinally *in situ* thereby causing reorientation. Eventually the tree reattains the erect habit. Recovery occurs in a few months for a woody seedling or only after many years for a forest tree (Fig. 4–1). Reaction wood is well known to wood users as a defect causing longitudinal shrinkage during the seasoning process. Boards with substantial amounts of reaction wood bow and warp.

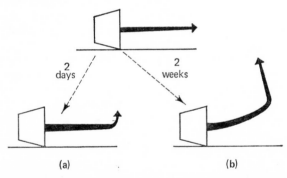

Fig. 4–1 Reorientation of a horizontally placed seedling. (a) There is rapid recovery of the shoot apex (primary tissues only) due to differential longitudinal growth on opposite sides of the young stem. (b) Reorientation of the woody stem occurs slowly by bending.

The wood produced from the vascular cambium is lignified and as such is inherently rigid and inextensible. Reorientation of the displaced woody stem or branch must therefore involve a process of bending. This is entirely different in nature than the growth movements of plant organs which have primary tissues only (e.g. *Avena* coleoptile) and in which reorientation occurs by differential longitudinal growth.

The reaction wood of arborescent angiosperms, *tension wood*, forms along the upper side of stems and branches and causes reorientation by longitudinal contraction *in situ*. The woolliness of portions of boards sawed from recently felled hardwood timber is directly related to the presence of this form of reaction wood. The fibres of tension wood resist being cut and project, as fragments, from the board surface, offering difficulties not only during sawing but also at later stages of finishing e.g., planing. Another serious difficulty caused by the presence of tension wood is end splitting of logs occurring immediately after felling, and resulting from release of severe internal stresses built up by this tissue.

Tension wood is characterized by a high cellulose and a low lignin content relative to normal wood. There are few vessel members and these are small in diameter (Plate 2a). Tension wood fibres, sometimes called gelatinous fibres, possess a thick, gel-like, inner layer of the secondary cell wall, the S(G) layer (Plate 2b). The S(G) layer may occur in addition to the usual three-layered secondary wall, or it may replace either the S_3 or the S_2 and S_3 layers (WARDROP, 1964b). The cellulose of the S(G) layer is oriented parallel to the long axis of the fibre (Plate 2c, d). Little or no lignin is present. In tension wood the higher and lower content of cellulose and lignin respectively derives largely from the chemical composition of the S(G) layer.

The reaction wood of gymnosperms, *compression wood*, forms along the *lower* side of tilted woody stems. Compression wood exists in stems and branches in a state of longitudinal compression, and is thought to effect reorientation by expansion *in situ*. In softwoods, compression wood is a serious defect, being harder and denser than normal wood, and possessing poor nail holding capacity (WESTING, 1965).

Reaction wood is generally considered to be an abnormal wood not usually associated with normal tree growth. However, there are obvious exceptions. For example, the terminal shoot of *Tsuga canadensis* (eastern hemlock, eastern North America) characteristically droops and swings in the wind at the beginning of the growing season, and only later on does gradual upward bending occur, and this is associated with the development of compression wood (MERGEN, 1958). The seasonal growth habit of the leader is characteristic of the species; it is genetically determined and, as such, compression wood formation here is a normal aspect of tree growth.

Tracheids of compression wood differ considerably in structure from those of normal wood. They are round in transverse section and readily identified by the presence of conspicuous intercellular spaces. The secondary cell wall consists of an outer S_1 and a thick inner S_2 layer. Unlike the tracheid of normal wood (Chapter 2) cellulose of the S_2 layer is oriented at an angle of about $45°$ to the long cellular axis. The S_3 wall layer is absent.

The lignin content of compression wood is higher than that of normal wood whereas the cellulose content is lower. This is due to the construction of the compression wood tracheid. The *outermost* (away from the lumen) portion of the S_2 layer contains very little cellulose and a considerable quantity of lignin. This lignin-rich zone is termed the $S_2(L)$ (Fig. 4-2). The ultrastructure and chemical composition of the $S_2(L)$ layer has recently been examined in *Larix* (CÔTÉ et al., 1968). Small blocks of wood are delignified by acidified sodium chlorite, a reagent which oxidizes lignin. Cell wall polysaccharides are largely unaffected by this treatment. From other blocks of wood cellulose is removed by controlled exposure to hydrofluoric and hydrochloric acids. Lignin is stable in acid whereas cell wall polysaccharides including cellulose are readily hydrolyzed. Examination by electron microscopy of wood from which cellulose has been removed by hydrolysis shows that the S_2 wall layer is structurally coherent. In particular, the $S_2(L)$ persists as a very dense lignin residue. On the other

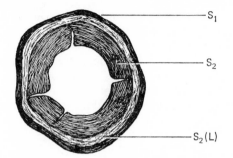

Fig. 4–2 Drawing showing the distribution of microfibrils in a transverse section of a completely delignified compression wood tracheid. See text for explanation. (After Fig. 12, p. 28, CÔTÉ et al., 1968.)

hand, examination of specimens from which lignin has been extracted shows that cellulose occurs in the $S_2(L)$ but in very small amounts. The cellulose residue of this wall layer is very porous (Fig. 4–2). This investigation shows conclusively that the $S_2(L)$ of compression wood tracheids consists of a very loose cellulosic framework embedded in a very dense lignin matrix.

4.2   Causes of reaction wood formation

Plant anatomists at the beginning of this century postulated that the formation of reaction wood was a response to asymmetric longitudinal stress. It was assumed that tensile stress along the upper side of a tilted angiosperm stem caused the differentiation of tension wood. On the other hand, in gymnosperms, compression wood formed along the lower side of bent stems where compressive stress was maximal. The concept of reaction wood as a stress response received some support from early workers concerned with the effect of physical factors on the differentiation of plant tissue. Jaccard (SINNOTT, 1960) studied the interesting phenomenon which occurred when a small root passed over a larger woody root and was subsequently placed under tension by the growth in diameter of the latter. The cell walls were thicker in the xylem elements of the root under tension than in similar cells of non-stressed controls.

However, additional experiments suggest that reaction wood is formed in response to a gravitational stimulus. For example, if the stem of a young hardwood is bent in a vertical loop and maintained in this orientation, tension wood forms on the upper side of the stem both at the top and bottom of the loop (see WARDROP, 1964b). Thus, reaction wood develops along the *upper* side irrespective of whether the looped stem is under a longitudinal tensile or compressive stress. The direct influence of gravity on the formation of reaction wood is also seen in experiments in which woody stems are placed in orientations other than the erect habit. Reaction wood is usually absent from stems maintained in the erect position, but forms readily when the axis is deflected by as little as one or two degrees from the vertical. The amount of reaction wood formed in stems is correlated with the degree of lean from the vertical direction.

Although gravitational stimulus accounts for the formation of reaction wood in stems, the case for branches is more complex. SINNOTT (1960) observed that compression wood formed along either the lower or upper side in branches of *Pinus strobus* bent downward or upward respectively

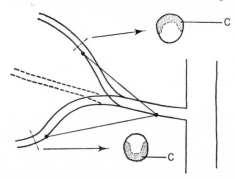

Fig. 4–3   Compression wood (C) is produced along either the lower or upper side of branches bent downward or upward respectively. In similar experiments with angiosperms the position of reaction wood is reversed. (From *Plant Morphogenesis* (Fig. 16–7) by E. W. SINNOTT. Copyright 1960 by the McGraw-Hill Book Company, Inc. Used with permission of McGraw-Hill Book Company.)

(Fig. 4–3). In these experiments, the position of compression wood in the branch is not constant with respect to gravitational force. Rather, compression wood appears to form on either the top or bottom of the branch so as to cause a recovery toward the former (undisturbed) orientation. Experiments such as this suggest that gravitational stimulus is only one of the factors involved in the induction of reaction wood in branches. Certain intrinsic factors must also be operative.

The formation of reaction wood in branches may be interpreted in terms of plagiotropism. Accordingly, the orientation movements of woody branches and more precisely the asymmetry of reaction wood formation derive from the interaction or two opposing forces: (1) an intrinsic force (epinasty) which drives the branch downward and (2) negative geotropism by which the branch tends toward a more vertical position. Epinasty in most plants is thought to relate to the physiological activities of the terminal bud of the stem on which the branch is inserted. Reorientation movements of the uppermost branch of *Liquidambar styraciflua* (sweetgum) are illustrative of the plagiotropism occurring during tree growth (Fig. 4-4). Two-year-old seedlings are decapitated and grown for three months either in an erect position or on a horizontal klinostat (WARDROP, 1964b). In the erect plants the uppermost branch shows strong negative geotropism and tension wood forms along the upper side (Fig. 4-4b). In plants grown on the klinostat there is only a very slight downward reorientation; no tension wood is formed (Fig. 4-4c). The absence of substantial reorientation in the latter is explicable in terms of removal of both gravitational and epinastic stimuli by the klinostat and decapitation treatments respectively.

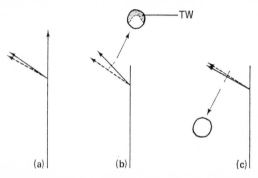

Fig. 4-4 Plagiotropic movement of the uppermost branch in *Liquidambar styraciflua*. (a) In erect, intact controls there is a slight movement toward the main axis. (b) In decapitated controls (epinasty removed) there is strong upward reorientation correlated with the formation of tension wood (TW) on the upper side. (c) In decapitated plants rotated on a horizontal klinostat (constant direction of gravitational force eliminated) the branch undergoes a slight downward movement but no tension wood is developed. Final branch position = solid line. (After Fig. 31, p. 441, WARDROP, 1964b. Copyright Academic Press.)

In erect decapitated *Liquidambar* only the epinastic factor is missing and the branch responds to gravitational stimulus by the formation of tension wood along the upper side, resulting in a strong, negative geotropic reorientation. Thus, the opposed epinastic and geotropic forces appear to govern the deposition of reaction wood on one or the other side of the axis. Thimann (WARDROP, 1964b) discusses this concept in terms of a unifying hormonal concept.

In recent years there has been considerable interest in the elucidation of the hormonal basis of reaction wood formation. Nečesaný (WARDROP, 1964b) reports a higher level of auxin along the lower side of *branches* of *Populus* and *Pinus* maintained in the horizontal position. In horizontally placed *stems* of *Populus* there is also an asymmetry of auxin concentration in the ratio 40/60 between the top and lower sides respectively (LEACH and WAREING, 1967). Thus, in both angiosperms and gymnosperms auxin is found in greater quantity on the lower side of bent stems and branches. However, the reaction wood of gymnosperms forms along the side where auxin concentration is high, whereas the reaction wood of angiosperms develops where the auxin level is low.

There is direct experimental evidence that the development of compression wood in stems is an auxin mediated response. Application of α-naphthalene acetic acid (NAA) in lanolin to erect stems of *Pinus* results in the formation of compression wood where otherwise only normal wood occurs (WARDROP, 1965). Compression wood is formed both above and below the site of auxin treatment, and when auxin is applied unilaterally there occurs within a few weeks a bending of the woody stem in the direction *away* from the treatment site.

By contrast several experiments suggest that the formation of tension wood is a response to an auxin *deficiency*. Nečesaný (WARDROP, 1964b) applied IAA in lanolin either to the top or to the bottom side of stems of *Populus* bent in the horizontal position. Basal application has little effect on the development of tension wood along the opposite side. However, application of auxin at the same concentration along the upper side drastically inhibits the formation of tension wood. Recently, it has been demonstrated that tension wood can be experimentally induced in vertical stems of *Acer* by treatment with an inhibitor of polar auxin transport, 2, 3, 5-triiodobenzoic acid (TIBA). A complete ring of tension wood forms in erect stems locally below the site of TIBA treatment (Plate 3). If however, auxin is applied simultaneously with TIBA, little or no tension wood is differentiated, indicating that tension wood does form in response to an auxin deficiency.

The development of reaction wood in stems and branches thus appears explicable in terms of an auxin level mechanism. The reaction wood of gymnosperms forms in response to a high level of auxin whereas the reverse is true for angiosperms. In tilted woody *stems* auxin accumulates along the lower side. Reaction wood then forms along the lower side in gymnosperms and the upper side in angiosperms. In branches the occurrence of reaction wood may be interpreted on the basis of two opposing forces, negative geotropism and epinasty, which drive auxin to the lower and upper sides respectively. The interaction of these forces determines the distribution of auxin in the branch, the site of formation of reaction wood and the direction of reorientation. For example, in a branch bent upward it is likely that there is a net accumulation of auxin along the top side, because gravitational force is less asymmetrically applied and thus less effective in driving auxin toward the lower side. At the same time epinasty (undiminished) continues to drive auxin toward the upper side so that there is net accumulation there. Accordingly, in branches of *Pinus* bent vertically, auxin accumulates along the upper side effecting the formation of compression wood, and causing a reorientation of the branch downward toward its undisturbed position (Fig. 4–3). It remains for future work to test this concept on an experimental basis.

Significant contributions are needed on the mechanism by which auxin is transported to one or the other side of thick woody stems and branches. In addition no satisfactory explanation is available as to why the angiosperms and gymnosperms have evolved such dissimilar reorientation mechanisms both on structural and physiological grounds. In *Drimys aromatica*, a primitive angiosperm with vessel-less wood, reaction wood resembles that of gymnosperms but unlike the latter it forms characteristically on the upper side of the deflected stem (for references see WESTING, 1965). Studies on this species would be of considerable evolutionary interest for here the control mechanism governing reaction wood development combines obvious angiosperm and gymnosperm components.

The Bark   5

5.1 Structure of the bark

Bark has been of economic importance for many centuries. Roman swimmers long ago employed cork floats made from the bark of *Quercus suber*, the cork oak tree (SCHERY, 1952). In addition, the fibres found in the bark of trees were utilized by the Chinese in papermaking long before a suitable technology was developed for the pulping of wood.

The formation of the bark begins only after the cessation of stem extension. The stem of the twig which is now fully elongated is covered by an epidermis overlying a parenchymatic cortex. The epidermis and cortex are soon placed under tangential strain caused by the initiation of the vascular cambium and the onset of radial growth. For a time the epidermal and cortical tissues may undergo radial growth themselves by a combination

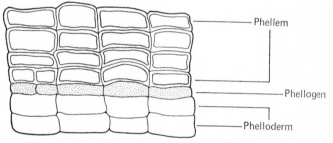

Fig. 5-1   Transverse section showing the phellogen and its radially aligned derivatives on the outside (phellem = cork) and inside (phelloderm).

of anticlinal division and tangential cell expansion. However, a new protective tissue system, the periderm, arises shortly thereafter, usually in the outer cortex. For example, the outer layer of cortical parenchyma may become meristematic all around the circumference of the stem. Cell division is restricted largely to the periclinal plane and a new lateral meristem, the *phellogen*, is initiated. Initials of the phellogen give rise to a large number of derivatives to the outside, the *cork* or *phellem*, and to a lesser number of cells to the inside, the *phelloderm*. The phellogen together with its two derivative tissues constitute a periderm (Fig. 5-1). Derivatives of the phellogen, like those of the vascular cambium are aligned in radial rows. However, unlike the vascular cambium, more derivatives of the phellogen are produced toward the outside than to the inside. In addition, the cells of the phellogen itself are all alike. There is no axial and radial system of cells in the periderm.

Cork is a non-living tissue that protects the underlying living portions of the trunk and branches. Cork cells are air filled and closely packed. As such cork is an excellent insulator and is utilized in the manufacture of insulation board. In addition to the usual cell wall constituents, such as cellulose and lignin, cork contains large quantities of *wax* and *suberin*. Suberin is a heterogeneous polyester consisting of a number of hydroxyfatty acids such as phellonic $HO—CH_2—(CH_2)_{20}—COOH$ and phloionic $HOOC—(CH_2)_7—(CHOH)_2—(CH_2)_7—COOH$ acid. Suberin and wax together make the phellem impervious to most liquids (consider bottle cork) and are responsible for the protective nature of the periderm.

The first periderm is usually replaced by sequent periderms developed in the underlying tissue of the bark. There are a few exceptions, e.g. beech, where the original periderm may be retained for a century. Here the phellogen obviously keeps pace with the girth growth of the xylem cylinder by multiplicative anticlinal division. In most trees however, the initial periderm is soon followed by those which arise from parenchyma located successively deeper in the bark, first in the cortex, later in the primary phloem and then finally in the secondary phloem. These sequent periderms usually have the shape of curved shells with their ends pointed outward (Fig. 2–1). As the cork of each new periderm matures, the cortex or phloem isolated by its formation becomes cut off from the underlying living tissue and soon dies. Bark of this type, termed *scale bark*, is later exfoliated in small pieces reflecting the organization of the successive periderms themselves. The term *rhytidome* refers to the *outer bark*, consisting of a series of periderms plus the variable amount of tissue (cortex and later phloem) isolated by their formation. In *Sequoia sempervirens* (redwood, western USA) where successive periderms are coherent the rhytidome of the trunk may become up to 30 centimetres thick.

The term *inner bark* refers to all tissues from the outer face of the cambial zone up to the innermost periderm. The inner bark includes both the *functioning* and *non-functioning phloem*. The former is active in the translocation of sugars. By contrast, the non-functional phloem is no longer active in translocation, but it does contain living axial and ray parenchyma. The non-functional phloem is placed under tangential strain as new xylem and phloem are differentiated from the vascular cambium beneath. Tangential strain is relieved (1) by removal of the outermost non-functioning phloem by periderm formation and subsequent exfoliation and (2) by *dilation growth* of axial and ray parenchyma. For example, in maples and elms the axial parenchyma of the non-functioning phloem divides and expands tangentially thereby giving rise to dilation tissue that increases the circumference of the outer surface of the inner bark (ESAU, 1969).

There is considerable difference in the surface texture of bark even in trees of the same family. Comparison of *Fagus sylvatica* and *Quercus robur*, members of the Fagaceae, shows that the bark of the former, beech, is smooth (phellem shed in very fine fragments) while that of oak is fissured and scaly. In beech, where the superficial smooth periderm is retained for many years, tangential strain in the cortex and secondary phloem is relieved by a considerable amount of dilation growth. On the other hand in oak there is less dilation growth and the outer part of the inner bark is consistently removed by sequential periderm formation. WHITMORE (1963) suggests that the surface pattern of bark is related to the rate of phloem production. Where the rate is high, e.g. oak, and tangential strain in the inner bark is not relieved by sufficient dilation growth, a considerable amount of tissue is removed by successive periderm formation leading to the development of a scaly bark. In trees with smooth bark little tissue is sloughed because the rate of phloem production is low and dilation growth is high. Other investigators point out that while Whitmore's suggestion is interesting, his measurements on the rate of phloem production are based not on direct observation, but rather on assumptions of uncertain validity (see ESAU, 1969, p. 242).

5.2   Developmental studies

The vascular cambium and phellogen are dissimilar not only in terms of the derivative tissues produced but also with regard to the timing of their initiation and to their seasonal pattern of activity. For example, the vascular cambium of *Sassafras* is initiated in twigs during their first growing season. However, the first periderm is formed some years later and then only discontinuously around the stem and branches (WEISS, 1906). In trees grown outdoors near New Haven, Connecticut (USA), the phellogen arises initially on the top side of branches and also on the south side of erect stems. Three or four years pass before the first periderm completely forms around the circumference of the stem or branch. Thus, periderm is initiated considerably later than the vascular cambium and environmental factors like insolation are involved in its induction.

In large branches of black locust in Israel, the phellogen is active during April and again in July. At all other times of the year it remains dormant (WAISEL et al., 1967). On the other hand, activity in the vascular cambium of the same branch begins in early March and continues in an uninterrupted manner up to the end of August. In experiments with three-year-old black locust seedlings grown under a high temperature, long-day regime, the phellogen is inactive even though the vascular cambium is active and height growth is underway. This suggests that the phellogen remains inactive under conditions in which shoot growth is stimulated and where presumably a high level of auxin and gibberellin is expected (§ 1.3).

Further experiments with black locust show that in seedlings treated with sprays of an auxin or a gibberellin the phellogen is initiated in internodes farther away from the shoot apex than in control plants (ARZEE et al., 1968). It may be that the hormones produced during extension growth of the shoot (auxins, gibberellins) are inhibitory with regard to periderm formation (CUTTER, 1969). On the other hand, other hormones may be specifically active in promoting the development of periderm. A recent experiment shows that a cytokinin (benzyladenine) promotes the formation of a periderm-like tissue in roots of *Ophioglossum petiolatum,* a fern, in which a periderm is normally never developed (PETERSON, 1971). Treatment with benzyladenine induces the outer cortical cells to undergo periclinal division leading to the production of distinct radial rows of derivatives. Histochemical tests show that the cell walls of the periderm-like tissue are suberized. Although a phellogen itself is not induced by benzyladenine, this interesting experiment does suggest an avenue of future work in plants where periderm formation is a normal occurrence.

5.3   The cork oak

Bottle cork and the cork utilized in the production of bottle cap liners, insulation board, linoleum and tile are all derived from the conspicuous, ring-like, periderm of the cork oak, *Quercus suber.* In this tree, a cork layer several inches thick is developed from the phellogen in as little as 8 or 10

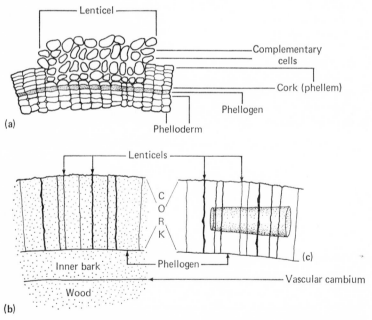

Fig. 5–2 (a) Diagram showing the loose texture of the phellem (complementary cells) of a lenticel. (b) Transverse section of bark of *Quercus suber* showing the cork, phellogen, inner bark and wood. Lenticels appear as fine lines traversing the cork. (c) Cork stoppers are cut from sheets of cork at right angles to the surface so that lenticels run horizontally across the stopper.

years. In most other trees however, the cork layer is thin and the rhytidome consists largely of isolated secondary phloem.

Special care must be taken not to damage the living tissue beneath the phellogen during the removal of the cork layer from the trunk and largest branches of the cork oak. A vertical slit is made in the bark with a curved axe or saw. Using pry levers, the cork is then stripped as a cylinder from the underlying inner bark. Initially the exposed surface of the stripped trunk or branch is pink-tan; but then, as drying occurs the surface colour changes almost to black (METCALF, 1947). A new complete phellogen develops deep within the inner bark shortly after stripping. Evidence of phellogen˙activity is seen shortly thereafter when vertical cracks appear in the black trunk surface revealing the light-tan colour of the new cork layer directly below. The second layer is of better quality than the first and is ready for stripping about 10 years later. Cork of the highest quality (uniform texture) is derived from the third to the sixth stripping and is utilized in the production of bottle stoppers.

The manufacture of cork stoppers for vintage wines deserves special comment. The cork of *Quercus suber*, like that of other trees, is not completely impervious to the outside environment. Rather, there is need for gas exchange (CO_2 and O_2) between the respiring tissues of the inner bark and the air without. This is facilitated by lenticels, small local areas of the periderm where the cork cells are only loosely coherent and intercellular spaces are abundant (Fig. 5–2). Now in cork oak, where lenticels several inches long pass from the phellogen to the outer bark surface, it is essential that cork stoppers be cut not from the surface of the cork layer, but rather at right angles to the surface (SCHERY, 1952). In this manner the lenticels run horizontally across the cork stopper and not vertically wherein leakage would most certainly occur (Fig. 5–2).

Roots

6.1 Morphology

The root system of a forest tree necessarily penetrates a large volume of soil. In addition to an obvious supportive function, the roots must be sufficiently active in producing root hairs early in the spring so that adequate water and minerals are available at the onset of rapid shoot growth. The control of root growth in trees is a complex process affected not only by the shoot (e.g. seasonal availability of photosynthate) but also by many fluctuating external factors in the soil including temperature, and the distribution of nutrients and moisture.

In trees with large seeds the first seedling root, the *tap root*, grows quickly to a great depth and becomes woody. Tap roots of mesquite (*Prosopis*) and locust (*Robinia*) are sometimes found 15 and 20 metres respectively below the soil surface (LYR and HOFFMANN, 1967). During periods of water stress tap roots are of considerable adaptive advantage in tree growth because moisture is still available even though the water table is very low.

Not all woody roots are located deep in the soil. A shallow excavation in the floor of a dense forest reveals numerous rope-like, woody roots, the *horizontal roots*, growing in the upper foot of soil. These roots extend outward from the trunk sometimes for a distance much greater than the radius of the tree crown. Spruce has many shallow roots of the horizontal type.

Many intensively branched, non-woody, *fine roots* arise from the larger tap and horizontal roots. The importance of fine roots derives from their large aggregate surface area. In a one-year-old root system of black locust, the roots of a diameter class less than 1.0 mm comprise only 16% of the total weight but 93% of the total root length and an even higher proportion of the surface area (LYR and HOFFMANN, 1967). Because of their large surface area, the fine roots of trees are necessarily important in the uptake of water and minerals from the soil.

Based on characteristics of diameter, elongation rate and longevity, fine roots are conveniently divided into two classes, long roots and short roots (WILCOX, 1964). The framework of the root system of a forest tree is built up by relatively thick (up to 2.0 mm), fast growing *long roots*. Later on these roots may become permanent with the development of a vascular cambium and a secondary plant body. Long roots give rise to a variable number of thin branches, the *short roots*, which have a longevity of only one or two seasons and are often mycorrhizal. Short roots in red pine have a diameter of about 0.40 mm (WILCOX, 1964).

Long roots themselves may be subdivided into *pioneer* or *mother roots*. The former refers to the thicker fast growing roots that penetrate a large volume of soil and quickly establish the framework of the root system.

These roots are only infrequently branched. On the other hand, mother roots are somewhat thinner, grow at a slower rate and give rise to a multitude of short roots.

Heterogeneity in the fine roots system is an obvious advantage in tree growth. If the quality of the soil is poor (e.g. an impoverished sandy soil) there is an adaptive advantage to the development of long roots of the pioneer type. The root system is capable of quickly penetrating a large volume of soil in search of water and nutrients. However, where a soil horizon is locally rich, the development of mother roots with short branches is promoted, leading to the intensive exploitation of the available moisture and minerals.

6.2   Seasonal growth

In the temperate latitudes there are some interesting differences in the seasonal course of shoot and root growth. Extension growth of fine roots in some trees for example begins earlier in the spring and lasts later into the autumn than growth in the shoot (LYR and HOFFMANN, 1967). In addition, the percentage of fine roots actively growing at any one time shows a very distinct seasonal pattern.

Techniques for studying root growth in forest trees are simple but necessarily laborious. Horizontal roots can be traced outward from the trunk to their ultimate branches. In this process long roots growing several inches below the soil surface are carefully exposed all along their length up to the root tip. The position of the latter is 'marked' simply by placing a peg off to one side (STEVENS, 1931). The front edge of the peg records the foremost position of the root tip. The root is covered with soil for a week or two and then the tip is again re-exposed. Extension growth is measured with a caliper placed between the edge of the peg and the new location of the root tip. This procedure may be repeated many times during the growing season without injury to the root. Growing and non-growing roots are easily distinguished by the white and brown colours of their root tips respectively.

The long roots of 4 to 5-year old white pine on New Hampshire (Eastern USA) sites are active from mid-April to early November (STEVENS, 1931). However, the proportion of actively extending roots varies at different times throughout the season (Fig. 6–1). Two peaks of root growth are observed. The first occurs in mid-May when nearly all roots are active whereas the second is in the early autumn at which time more than half of the roots are elongating. At the beginning of August between 60 and 80% of the roots excavated are non-growing as evidenced by their brown tips. Mid-summer inactivity is likely associated with high temperatures and desiccation in the upper soil horizons where these roots grow.

A similar seasonal pattern is obtained if the daily growth increment of actively extending roots only is measured (Fig. 6–2). Maximum daily

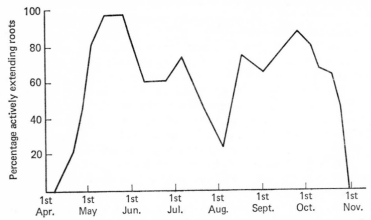

Fig. 6–1 Seasonal course of root growth in white pine. The percentage of roots which are actively extending is high in the mid-spring and again in early autumn. Most roots are inactive in the mid-summer. (After Plate 3, p. 31, STEVENS, 1931.)

growth of active roots occurs in the late spring and again in the early autumn with a mid-summer decline in between. Examination of Fig. 6–2 shows that the first surge of root growth coincides with the rapid burst of height

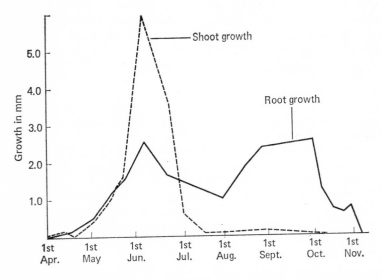

Fig. 6–2 Diagram showing average daily extension for growing roots only. The growth rate of active roots declines in the mid-summer. Root and shoot growth follow distinct seasonal patterns. (After Plate 6, p. 45, STEVENS, 1931.)

growth in the late spring. But from here on the course of root and shoot growth in white pine is divergent. Only a small amount of shoot growth occurs in the late summer and this is apparently associated with maturation of the terminal bud (STEVENS, 1931). By contrast, at the same time and later in the autumn roots show intense elongation suggesting that root and shoot growth may be autonomous. On the other hand, shading and pruning experiments indicate that the availability of photosynthate produced in the shoot strongly affects the growth of roots (LYR and HOFFMANN, 1967).

The seasonal course of root growth in forest trees may be studied by less laborious techniques. One very useful method is based on the pruning of horizontal roots (LYFORD and WILSON, 1966). The severed end of the root attached to the stem is wrapped in moist soil and within 2 to 3 weeks numerous fine roots are regenerated from the cut woody root. Instead of allowing regeneration to occur simply in a wrapping of soil, the severed horizontal root is firmly affixed to the bottom of a long, narrow wooden tray and is covered with a thin layer of moist soil. New roots develop in the plane of the tray and the effects of soil composition, temperature, and other environmental factors on root growth are then easily studied. The technique is carried one step further with the construction of a building called a *rhizotron* (LYFORD and WILSON, 1966). Here a trench like excavation in the forest floor next to a large tree is covered with an inexpensive shelter. Fine roots developed from severed horizontal roots along the side of the trench are grown 'indoors' in trays under controlled laboratory conditions. Lyford and Wilson report that the fine roots of red maple present in unheated trays in a rhizotron remain inactive during the cold winter months (November to April) in Petersham, Massachusetts (USA). However, if the trays are kept warm (20 °C) the fine roots grow continuously at the rate of 5 to 10 mm per day throughout the winter even though the aerial portion of the tree is dormant.

Similar results are reported for saplings of white pine transferred from outdoor conditions into a warm greenhouse in late October, at which time root tips are normally becoming inactive and turning brown (STEVENS, 1931). During the next four months under favourable greenhouse conditions some of these roots resume growth. One root is reported to have grown more than 22.5 centimetres. At the same time the shoot is inactive since rest is not broken by winter chilling. These experiments suggest that root growth in trees is to some extent independent of shoot control. Furthermore, the growth of roots in the winter in warm trays in the rhizotron or in a warm greenhouse indicates that in roots, unlike shoots, there is an absence of endogenous rest. Growth is continuous so long as temperature, moisture, and nutritional factors are not rate limiting.

6.3   Secondary growth

Long roots become a permanent part of the root system through the development of a vascular cambium and the formation of secondary vascular tissues. Although the vascular cambium and its derivative tissues in roots and stems are for the most part structurally similar there are some interesting differences in the mode of initiation of this lateral meristem in these very different organs. It will be recalled that in stems of dicotyledonous angiosperms, the vascular cambium is initiated in the procambium of the primary vascular bundles which are located in a somewhat peripheral position in the stem. By contrast in roots, where the primary vascular tissue exists as a central core, the vascular cambium is deep seated in origin.

The arrangement of the primary xylem in roots is referred to as *diarch*, *triarch*, *tetrarch*, etc., depending on the number of radial poles present (see Fig. 7–2 in GEMMELL, 1969). The xylem at the poles is the first to mature and is called *protoxylem*. Differentiation in the more centrally located *metaxylem* is completed somewhat later. Primary phloem occurs in discrete strands on the perimeter of the xylem core at positions between adjacent protoxylem poles. In roots in which a vascular cambium will be formed, a layer of procambium remains between the phloem strands and the xylem. The procambium is discontinuous around the xylem since each protoxylem pole abuts directly upon the *pericycle*. This layer surrounds the entire cylinder of primary xylem and phloem and it, in turn, is surrounded by the cortex.

The vascular cambium originates from the procambium of a young root as a series of discontinuous layers on the inner face of each primary phloem strand (ESAU, 1965). Successive periclinal division in each cambial layer soon produces a radially aligned series of derivatives. The xylem core then gradually assumes a cylindrical outline as the concavities between adjacent protoxylem poles are filled in with secondary xylem. Periclinal division soon occurs in the pericycle, first locally opposite the protoxylem poles, and later on throughout the entire layer. This leads to the formation of a thickened pericycle with radially aligned cells. The innermost periclinally dividing cells of the pericycle bordering on each protoxylem pole join with the cambial cells on both sides giving rise to a vascular cambium that is now continuous over the entire xylem cylinder. Thick seasonal increments of xylem and phloem are produced by the vascular cambium for many years, especially in the tapering roots close to the trunk. The wood of roots is commonly less dense than trunkwood owing to the presence in the former of fibres and tracheids of larger diameter.

In roots of pear the thickened pericycle for a time keeps pace with the expansion of the underlying cylinder of secondary vascular tissue (ESAU, 1943). After some tangential expansion, the outermost pericycle cells become suberized thereby assuming a protective function. By this time the overlying cortex and epidermis are crushed and split away. Later on a periderm develops from an inner layer of the proliferated pericycle.

The initiation of secondary growth in roots is controlled by the interaction of hormonal and metabolic factors. In excised roots of radish, a balanced mixture of an auxin (IAA), a cytokinin (kinetin), a cyclitol (myo-inositol) and sucrose set in motion the sequence leading to the induction and maximal activity of the vascular cambium (TORREY and LOOMIS, 1967). In order to be effective the chemical mixture must be applied by means of a narrow glass tube fitted onto the basal end of the root. This suggests that the initiation of secondary growth in roots is normally regulated by stimuli moving downward from the shoot.

7.1 The origin of the arborescent habit

The initiation of the cambial meristem and the formation of rigidified secondary tissues, especially the lignified xylem, were prerequisites to the emergence of the arborescent habit. We will consider initially a series of Devonian plants, which though not necessarily related phylogenetically, do nevertheless suggest the evolutionary development of tissue systems that occurred from the herbaceous to the arborescent habit. The simplest

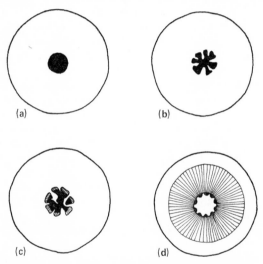

Fig. 7–1 Transverse sections of stems of Devonian plants showing the organization of the xylem during the transition from the herbaceous to the arborescent habit. **(a)** *Rhynia*. A solid core of primary xylem. **(b)** *Asteroxylon*. The primary xylem is somewhat dissected. **(c)** *Schizopodium*. Tracheids in radial rows occur at the edges of the lobed xylem. **(d)** *Callixylon*. The secondary xylem is massive. Primary xylem exists as a ring of discrete bundles surrounding a central pith. Solid = primary xylem. Crosshatched = secondary xylem.

vascular plants of the Palaeozoic, represented by *Rhynia* of the Psilophyta, grew only by the activities of the apical meristem and possessed a vascular system of simple organization (Fig. 7–1a). Examination of a transverse section of the leafless stem revealed a small, solid core of vascular tissue (xylem and phloem) termed the *protostele*. The stem was slender and in *R. gwynne-vaughani* grew to a height of about 0.2 metre. In *Asteroxylon*, a psilophyte or perhaps a primitive lycopod, with a monopodial stem bearing small leaves, the primary xylem was noticeably lobed and somewhat more massive (Fig. 7–1b). The largest stems of *Asteroxylon* attained a height of half a metre and a thickness of one centimetre *Schizopodium*, a leafless ally of the psilophytes of the Mid-Devonian, provided the first indication of secondary tissue development. The xylem of the protostele was lobed, and unlike that of *Asteroxylon*, the marginal tracheids of the lobes were arranged in radial rows, suggesting the presence of a lateral meristem (Fig. 7–1c). Apparently there was no true vascular cambium since the marginal tracheids were of irregular dimension and shape. Rather, the meristem which gave rise to the radially aligned tracheids in *Schizopodium* was probably transitional between the procambium and the vascular cambium.

A true vascular cambium appeared initially in *Tetraxylopteris*, a progymnosperm of the Middle Devonian (BECK, 1970). The progymnosperms were a group of seedless vascular plants which exhibited some structural characteristics similar to the gymnosperms and were thought to have given rise to the seed plants. The leaves of *Tetraxylopteris* were frond-like and the stem (about 6.5 centimetres thick) contained a gymnospermous-like wood. A massive arborescent habit developed later in *Archaeopteris* a progymnosperm of the Upper Devonian with large compound fronds up to a metre long. The woody trunk of *Archaeopteris* (Fig. 7–1d), known separately for many years under the stem genus *Callixylon*, was massive (some specimens up to 1.5 metres in diameter) and was characterized by an active vascular cambium. The wood of *Archaeopteris* (*Callixylon*) was simple in composition, consisting of only tracheids and parenchyma and as such it strongly resembled that of modern gymnosperms, especially *Araucaria*. Numerous groups of circular bordered pits were present in the radial walls of axial tracheids indicating the rapidity with which an efficient water conducting system developed in the sapwood of this arborescent species during the Devonian. The rays were from one to 3 or 4 cells wide and, in addition contained tracheids besides parenchyma (BECK, 1970).

One may wonder how the arborescent habit arose so rapidly in the Devonian. At best, we can only speculate that the erect woody stem evolved coincident with two archaic events: (1) the planation (flattening) and webbing of rapidly dichotomizing branches, leading to the development of leaves or fronds and (2) the development of biochemical mechanisms for the synthesis of phenylpropanoid molecules and their polymerization into primitive lignin-like substances.

The leaves of arborescent plants are a major source of the hormonal stimuli involved in internode elongation (e.g. *Ginkgo*) and in many of the steps in radial growth (Chapter 3). We may then speculate that the physiological systems necessary for the development of secondary tissue arose with the evolution of the primitive leaf. It has recently been demonstrated that the initiation of the vascular cambium itself is regulated by influences flowing from the shoot. This is shown clearly in grafting experiments between the reduced mutant and the normal form of tomato (CARUSO and CUTTER, 1970). When the mutant is grown in sterile culture the shoot apex, leaves and cotyledons are all absent and no vascular cambium forms in the hypocotyl. However, if a normal shoot tip is grafted onto the mutant, a vascular cambium is initiated in the hypocotyl and secondary xylem and phloem are formed. The shoot tip provides the hormones and metabolites necessary for the inception of this lateral meristem in the hypocotyl. In roots of radish an auxin and a cytokinin are absolute requirements for the initiation of a vascular cambium (TORREY and LOOMIS, 1967). Clearly then, the arborescent habit arose in the Devonian with the evolution of a similar biochemical mechanism controlling the initiation of a vascular cambium in an otherwise non-woody land plant.

Lignin was of central importance to the arborescent habit because of its stabilizing and rigidifying effect on other cell wall materials. The maintenance of the large, erect, arborescent plant body then depended to a large extent on the strength of the lignified secondary tissue systems. In an attempt to gain clues on the archaic events involved in the evolution of lignin, MANSKAYA and DROZDOVA (1968) analyzed the cell wall composition of modern representatives of several major groups of plants. Lignin was absent in algae and non-vascular land plants, e.g. the mosses. On the other hand, in the lycopods, ferns, gymnosperms and angiosperms, lignin building blocks were present in varying amounts (Table 2). It was evident,

Table 2 Presence of lignin in modern plant groups. Lignin residues (vanillin and syringaldehyde) obtained by oxidation with alkaline nitrobenzene. (Reprinted with permission from p. 100 of MANSKAYA and DROZDOVA, *Geochemistry of Organic Substances*, 1968, Pergamon Press.)

Material	Vanillin (%)
Fucus serratus (alga)	Trace
Polytrichum commune (moss)	Trace
Lycopodium (lycopod)	4.0
Alsophila australis (fern)	4.0
Araucaria bidwillii (gymnosperm)	6.0
Casuarina stricta (angiosperm)	2.0 (+ 1.0% Syringaldehyde)

therefore, that only the vascular land plants have achieved the capacity for lignin biosynthesis, and it was only in these groups that the arborescent habit is and/or was present. Furthermore, we may note that although the other major constituents of the plant cell wall, cellulose and hemicellulose, have likely been present since the Middle Precambrian (BARGHOORN, 1964), large erect plant forms arose only much later, in the Devonian, coincident with the development of mechanisms necessary for lignin synthesis.

7.2 Variations in the pattern of radial growth

By the early Carboniferous, the arborescent habit was also well developed in other groups of vascular plants including the Lycopsida and Sphenopsida. However, the secondary tissue systems in some groups had unusual structural features no longer found in extant trees. In the fossil Lycopsida secondary growth was based not on the preponderance of derivatives of the vascular cambium but rather on the extensive development of periderm-like tissue.

Lepidodendron was a large arborescent tree up to 30 metres tall with a tapering trunk at the top of which were dichotomizing branches bearing closely placed, spirally arranged leaves. Anatomical reconstruction showed that although there was a true vascular cambium, its activity must have

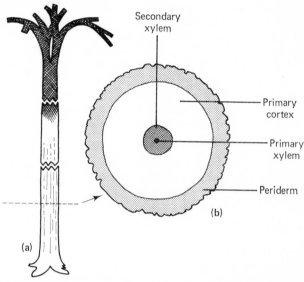

(a)

(b)

Secondary xylem

Primary cortex

Primary xylem

Periderm

Fig. 7-2 (a) Reconstruction of the trunk of *Lepidodendron*. The diamond shaped leaf cushions on the upper trunk are closely packed. (b) The trunk contains a massive periderm and a relatively inconspicuous secondary xylem. Leaf cushions have been sloughed from the lower trunk. (By permission from The Ontogeny of Carboniferous Arborescent Lycopsida, Figs. 68 and 75, EGGERT, 1961, *Palaeontographica*, 108B. Copyright, 1961 by E. Schweizer-bart'sche Verlagsbuchhandlung, Stuttgart.)

been limited and consequently only a small amount of secondary xylem was formed (Fig. 7-2). Not only was the percentage of wood in the trunk relatively low, but also the trachieds themselves were relatively thin-walled, and of less mechanical importance than similar cells of the pro-gymnosperms. Within the massive primary cortex there arose diffuse meristems in which successive periclinal divisions gave rise to radial rows of cells which in part composed the *secondary cortex* or *periderm*. Unlike the periderm of modern gymnosperms and angiosperms (Chapter 5), in *Lepidodendron* there was no evidence of a discrete phellogen (EGGERT, 1961), but rather the meristem was diffuse and its derivatives were sometimes fibrous, perhaps living, and certainly strongly supportive in function. Although the arborescent habit in *Lepidodendron* was highly successful in the Carboniferous, it failed later on, in times of environmental stress, probably because of the limited capacity for water transport by the meagre secondary xylem.

The developmental mechanisms operative in controlling radial growth in woody plants were well established by the end of the Palaeozoic. Consider for example, *Sphenophyllum*, a genus of the Sphenopsida which flourished in the Carboniferous. This was not a tree but rather a small, branched, woody, vine-like plant with definite nodes and internodes, that grew sometimes to a length of 10 metres, in the understory of Carboniferous forests. The protostele showed a triangular organization with three protoxylem poles and a centrally located metaxylem (DARRAH, 1968). The vascular cambium arose immediately outside the primary xylem and, at first, the resulting woody tissue assumed a triangular pattern (Plate 4) but later, as radial growth continued, a more cylindrical arrangement became prominent. The transition from a triangular to a cylindrical secondary xylem was brought about by an increased number of periclinal divisions and/or a greater enlargement of cambial derivatives in the regions opposite the metaxylem. In a similar manner a cylinder of wood is developed over an initially lobed core of primary xylem in the roots of some modern arborescent plants.

7·3 The influence of the long shoot

It will be recalled that the progymnosperm *Archaeopteris* was characterized by a massive secondary xylem. True arborescent gymnosperms (bearing naked seeds) arose in the Carboniferous and they are represented here by the genus *Cordaites* of the order Cordaitales. This was a large tree up to 30 metres tall with a massive but simply structured wood. The axial system of cells contained only tracheids whereas parenchyma of the radial system was organized as uniseriate (one cell wide) rays. Thus, the wood of *Cordaites* strongly resembled that of modern conifers. Branches bore long, spirally placed leaves with characteristic parallel venation (Fig. 7–3). Vegetative branches of *Cordaites* may be loosely defined as long shoots, that is, the shoot axis may be divided into *internodes* (where stem growth had previously occurred) and *nodes* (the point of attachment of a leaf). A definite indication of internode elongation in stems of *Cordaites* was revealed in pith casts by the occurrence of a series of cavities corresponding to the internodal portion of the stem (ARNOLD, 1947). In like manner, the terminal branches of *Archaeopteris* were long shoots (see diagram in BECK, 1970) in that the axis may also be described in terms of nodes and internodes.

Auxin is involved in the initiation of the vascular cambium and in various steps in radial growth. It is likely that the influence of the terminal shoot on radial growth is mediated at least in part by auxin produced in expanding leaves and internodes. Extending internodes, in particular, are known to produce large amounts of diffusible auxin (GUNCKEL and THIMANN, 1949). We may speculate then that the massive development of secondary xylem in Palaeozoic *Archaeopteris* and *Cordaites* is related to the long shoot

Fig. 7–3 Vegetative shoot of *Cordaites* showing parallel-veined leaves attached to the stem at regular intervals. The occurrence of shoots with extended internodes (long shoots) appears to be correlated with the development of a massive secondary xylem. (Diagram after DARRAH, 1960, Fig. 36, p. 159. Copyright 1960, The Ronald Press Company, New York.)

habit, a mode of shoot growth which persists within the gymnosperm line at the present time. The appearance of the long shoot may have provided the hormonal key which made possible the massive development of wood in these archaic plants. By contrast, in *Lepidodendron*, which is characterized by a continuous short shoot habit (note in Fig. 7–2 that there is no extension of the axis between successive leaf cushions), the secondary xylem shows only very limited development.

7.4   The origin of growth rings

In modern trees of the temperate latitudes and in some trees of the tropics the developmental sequence in the vascular cambium is rhythmic in that wood is produced in growth rings. The occurrence of rhythmic secondary growth is traced back to the Upper Devonian of New York in *Callixylon erianum* where weak growth rings are recorded (ARNOLD, 1947). JEFFREY (1917) made the interesting observation that in cordaitean wood from Prince Edward Island (46 °N) secondary growth is uniform while growth rings are present in similar wood obtained at a higher latitude in the north of England (54 °N, Lancashire). Rhythmic secondary growth is evident in the latter wood because of the decreased radial dimension of tracheids near the terminus of each increment. Although we cannot be sure as to what factors are responsible for these ancient rhythmic patterns, growth ring formation in the cordaitean wood from Lancashire may reflect a changing seasonal climate that probably occurred at the higher latitude. However, growth rings are found in cordaitean wood from other distant localities as for example in *Dadoxylon indicum*, a Palaeozoic cordaitean species from India. In the last period of the Palaeozoic, the Permian, and in the Mesozoic, growth rings, with well defined early and late wood, became worldwide in distribution, undoubtedly coinciding with a rhythmic seasonal environment including fluctuation in temperature and soil moisture. It is easy to see how a rhythmic external environment could affect wood formation since available photosynthate for cell wall thickening and auxin production for cell expansion are both subject to modification by environmental factors acting on shoot growth.

Growth ring production then appears to have initially arisen in the Palaeozoic and Mesozoic as a direct result of the action of external factors on the physiological systems of the growing shoot. The occurrence of growth rings today in a number of tropical trees however, suggests that the physiological mechanisms controlling periodic radial growth later became an intrinsic part of tree growth at least in some arborescent species (BARGHOORN, 1964). In like manner we have seen (Chapter 1) that the phenomenon of rest in the tropical tree *Oreopanax* may have originated at an earlier time while the genus was subject to a rhythmic, seasonal environment when it presumably grew at a higher latitude.

Future work based on the comparison of the structural features of fossil plants with the growth mechanisms operative in modern representatives will probably provide further clues on the mode and origin of tree growth in the past.

References

ALFIERI, F. J. and EVERT, R. F. (1968). *Am. J. Bot.*, **55**, 518–28.

ARNOLD, C. A. (1947). *An Introduction to Paleobotany*. New York, McGraw-Hill.

ARZEE, T., LIPHSCHITZ, N. and WAISEL, Y. (1968). *New Phytol.* **67**, 87–93.

BAILEY, I. W. (1920). *J. gen. Physiol.*, **2**, 519–33.

BANNAN, M. W. (1962). The Vascular Cambium and Tree-Ring Development. In *Tree Growth*. Edited by T. T. Kozlowski. New York, Ronald Press.

BARGHOORN, E. S. (1964). Evolution of Cambium in Geologic Time. In *The Formation of Wood in Forest Trees*. Edited by M. H. Zimmermann. New York, Academic Press.

BECK, C. B. (1970). *Biol. Rev.*, **45**, 379–400.

BORCHERT, R. (1969). *Am. J. Bot.*, **56**, 1033–41.

CARUSO, J. L. and CUTTER, E. G. (1970). *Am. J. Bot.*, **57**, 420–29.

CÔTÉ, W. A., JR., and DAY, A. C. (1969). Technical Publication No. 95. State University College of Forestry at Syracuse University, New York.

CÔTÉ, W. A., JR., DAY, A. C. and TIMELL, T. E. (1968). *Wood Sci. Technol.*, **2**, 13–37.

CRITCHFIELD, W. B. (1970). *Bot. Gaz.*, **131**, 150–62.

CUTTER, E. G. (1969). *Plant Anatomy*. Part 1. London, Edward Arnold.

DARRAH, E. L. (1968). *Palaeontographica, B.* **121**, 87–101.

DARRAH, W. C. (1960). *Principles of Paleobotany*. New York, Ronald Press.

DERR, W. F. and EVERT, R. F. (1967). *Am. J. Bot.*, **54**, 147–53.

DIGBY, J. and WAREING, P. F. (1966a). *Ann. Bot.* N. S., **30**, 539–48.

DIGBY, J. and WAREING, P. F. (1966b). *Ann. Bot.* N. S., **30**, 607–22.

EGGERT, D. A. (1961). *Palaeontographica, B.* **108**, 43–92.

ESAU, K. (1943). *Hilgardia*, **15**, 299–324.

ESAU, K. (1965). *Plant Anatomy*. New York, John Wiley.

ESAU, K. (1969). *The Phloem*. Berlin, Gebruder Borntraeger.

FERGUS, B. J., PROCTER, A. R., SCOTT, J. A. N. and GORING, D. A. I. (1969). *Wood Sci. Technol.*, **3**, 117–38.

FERGUSON, C. W. (1968). *Science*, **159**, 839–46.

FOSTER, A. S. (1931). *Am. J. Bot.*, **18**, 864–87.

FOSTER, A. S. (1932). *Am. J. Bot.*, **19**, 75–99.

GEMMELL, A. R. (1969). *Developmental Plant Anatomy*. London, Edward Arnold.

GLOCK, W. S. and AGERTER, S. R. (1962). Rainfall and Tree Growth. In *Tree Growth*. Edited by T. T. Kozlowski. New York, Ronald Press.

GORDON, J. C. and LARSON, P. R. (1968). *Pl. Physiol.*, Lancaster, **43**, 1617–24.

GREATHOUSE, D. C., LAETSCH, W. M., and PHINNEY, B. O. (1971). *Am. J. Bot.*, **58**, 281–86.

GUNCKEL, J. E. and THIMANN, K. V. (1949). *Am. J. Bot.*, **36**, 145–51.

HANSON, H. C. and BRENKE, B. (1926). *Bot. Gaz.*, **82**, 286–305.

JEFFREY, E. C. (1917). *The Anatomy of Woody Plants*. Chicago, University Press.

LARSON, P. R. (1962). Auxin Gradients and the Regulation of Cambial Activity. In *Tree Growth*. Edited by T. T. Kozlowski. New York, Ronald Press.

LEACH, R. W. A. and WAREING, P. F. (1967). *Nature, Lond.*, **214**, 1025–27.

LYFORD, W. H. and WILSON, B. F. (1966). *Harvard Forest Paper*, No 16. Petersham, Massachusetts.

LYR, H. and HOFFMANN, G. (1967). Growth Rates and Growth Periodicity of Tree Roots. In *Int. Rev. For. Res.*, **2**, Edited by J. A. Romberger and P. Mikola. New York, Academic Press.

MANSKAYA, S. M. and DROZDOVA, T. V. (1968). *Geochemistry of Organic Substances*. Translated, Edited by L. Shipiro and I. A. Breger. Oxford, Pergamon Press.

MERGEN, F. (1958). *For. Sci., Washington, D.C.*, **4**, 98–109.

METCALF, W. (1947). *Econ. Bot.*, **1**, 26–46.

MOREY, P. R. and CRONSHAW, J. (1968). *Protoplasma.* **65**, 287–313.

PARKE, R. V. (1959). *Am. J. Bot.*, **46**, 110–18.

PETERSON, R. L. (1971). *Ann. Bot.* N. S., **35**, 165–67.

PHILIPSON, W. R., WARD, J. M., and BUTTERFIELD, B. G. (1971). *The Vascular Cambium*. London, Chapman and Hall.

ROBARDS, A. W., DAVIDSON, E., and KIDWAI, P. (1969). *J. exp. Bot.*, **20**, 912–20.

ROELOFSEN, P. A. (1959). *The Plant Cell Wall*. Berlin, Gebruder Borntraeger.

ROMBERGER, J. A. (1963). *Meristems, Growth and Development in Woody Plants*. Washington, D.C., U.S. Dept. Agric.

RUBERY, P. H. and NORTHCOTE, D. H. (1968). *Nature, Lond.*, **219**, 1230–34.

SACHER, J. A. (1954). *Am. J. Bot.*, **41**, 749–59.

SCHERY, R. W. (1952). *Plants for Man*. Englewood Cliffs, Prentice Hall.

SCOTT, J. A. N., PROCTER, A. R., FERGUS, B. J. and GORING, D. A. I. (1969). *Wood Sci. Technol.*, **3**, 73–92.

SINNOTT, E. W. (1960). *Plant Morphogenesis*. New York, McGraw-Hill.

STEVENS, C. L. (1931). *Yale Univ. School Forestry Bull.* No. 32. New Haven, Connecticut.

TORREY, J. G. and LOOMIS, R. S. (1967). *Am. J. Bot.*, **54**, 1098–1106.

TUCKER, C. M. and EVERT, R. F. (1969). *Am. J. Bot.*, **56**, 275–84.

WAISEL, Y., LIPHSCHITZ, N. and ARZEE, T. (1967). *New Phytol.*, **66**, 331–35.

WARDROP, A. B. (1964a). The Structure and Formation of the Cell Wall in Xylem. In *The Formation of Wood in Forest Trees*. Edited by M. H. Zimmermann. New York, Academic Press.

WARDROP, A. B. (1964b). The Reaction Anatomy of Arborescent Angiosperms. In *The Formation of Wood in Forest Trees*. Edited by M. H. Zimmerman. New York, Academic Press.

WARDROP, A. B. (1965). The Formation and Function of Reaction Wood. In *Cellular Ultrastructure of Woody Plants*. Edited by W. A. Côté. Syracuse, University Press.

WAREING, P. F. (1951). *Physiologia Pl.*, **4**, 546–62.

WAREING, P. F. (1958). *Nature, Lond.*, **181**, 1744–45.

WAREING, P. F. (1969). Germination and Dormancy. In *The Physiology of Plant Growth and Development*. Edited by M. B. Wilkins. London, McGraw-Hill.

WAREING, P. F. and PHILLIPS, I. D. J. (1970). *The Control of Growth and Differentiation in Plants*. Oxford, Pergamon Press.

WEISS, H. F. (1906). *Bot. Gaz.*, **41**, 434–44.

WESTING, A. H. (1965). *Bot. Rev.*, **31**, 381–480.

WHITMORE, T. C. (1963). *New Phytol.*, **62**, 161–69.

WILCOX, H. (1964). Xylem in Roots of *Pinus resinosa* Ait. in Relation to Heterorhizy and Growth Activity. In *The Formation of Wood in Forest Trees*. Edited by M. H. Zimmermann. New York, Academic Press.

ZIMMERMANN, M. H. and BROWN, C. L. (1971). Trees: Structure and Function. New York, Springer-Verlag.